EP Language Arts 1
Workbook

This book belongs to:

_____

EP Language Arts 1 Workbook

Copyright © 2017   All rights reserved.

ISBN-13: 978-1548631499
ISBN-10: 1548631493

Second Edition: July 2017

About this Workbook

This is an offline workbook for Easy Peasy All-in-One Homeschool's Language Arts 1 course. We've modified and expanded upon the online activities and printable worksheets available at the Easy Peasy All-in-One Homeschool website (www.allinonehomeschool.com) so that your child can work offline if desired. Whether you use the online or offline versions, or a combination of both, your child will enjoy these supplements to the Easy Peasy Language Arts course.

How to use this Workbook

This workbook is designed to be used in conjunction with Easy Peasy's Language Arts 1 Parent's Guide. As you proceed through the Parent's Guide, use this workbook to exercise your child's language arts skills.

This workbook follows the EP online Language Arts course in sequential order, providing 180 daily activity worksheets which can replace online activities and printable worksheets. The daily worksheets are designed with the following guidelines in mind:

- ## To supplement daily lessons
  This workbook on its own supplements, but does not replace, EP's daily lessons. Be sure to check the daily lesson on the website or in the Parent's Guide before having your child do the workbook activities.

- ## To serve as an alternative to online activities
  This workbook serves as an alternative to the activities posted online, providing offline activities in sufficient quantities and varieties to challenge your child. When used in conjunction with the Parent's Guide, this workbook becomes a complete offline course.

Please note, in the various places where nouns are practiced, certain words like run, walk, fly, etc. are considered to be verbs. While there are instances where they can be nouns (you can go for a run, a fly can be a bug, etc.) this book assumes a more basic approach for this introductory level. If your child marks one of them as a noun, have a conversation with them to find out why.

Available Online

- The printable worksheets, a subset of this workbook, are available online.
- The solutions are on the website as well as in the Parent's Guide and are **not included** in this workbook.

Completion Chart for Lessons 1 - 45

#	Lesson	#	Lesson	#	Lesson
1	Long a/rhyming	16	Hard/soft s	31	Beginning/ending "sh"
2	Long a	17	Ending blends	32	Hard/soft "th"
3	Long e	18	Beginning blends	33	Wh sound
4	Long e	19	Ch sound	34	Thr/shr blends
5	Long i	20	Ck sound	35	Silent e
6	Long i	21	Story order	36	Main idea
7	Long o	22	Book report	37	Ending punctuation
8	Long o	23	Spelling "ot"	38	Capital I
9	Long u	24	Spelling "ot"	39	Is/are
10	Long u	25	Ordering sentences	40	Is/are
11	My information	26	Ordering sentences	41	Long/short a
12	Story order	27	Story writing	42	Long/short e
13	Spelling "an"	28	Story writing	43	Long/short i
14	Spelling "an"	29	Story writing	44	Long/short o
15	Story order	30	Story writing	45	Long/short u

Completion Chart for Lessons 46 - 90

46	Inference	61	Crazy sentences	76	Weather words
47	Punctuation	62	Punctuation	77	Describing
48	Inference	63	Punctuation	78	Describing
49	Picture order	64	Capitalization/ punctuation	79	Describing
50	Inference	65	Writing sentences	80	Describing
51	Ar blend	66	Knock, knock jokes	81	Silly story
52	Ir, ur, er blends	67	Describing	82	Describing
53	Or blend	68	Shape poem	83	Describing
54	Ire	69	Short story	84	Describing
55	Rhyming	70	Speech practice	85	Silly story
56	Alphabetical order	71	Beginning/ending letters	86	Repeating consonants
57	Alphabetical order	72	Vowel sounds	87	Descriptive sentences
58	Alphabetical order	73	Make a cartoon	88	Punctuation/ capitalization
59	Alphabetical order	74	Make a cartoon	89	Sounds words
60	Alphabetical order	75	Make a cartoon	90	Sounds words

Completion Chart for Lessons 91-135

91	Setting	106	Spelling/blending words	121	Nouns/spelling
92	Setting	107	Spelling	122	Proper nouns/ spelling
93	Setting	108	Letter picking	123	Proper nouns/ spelling
94	Setting	109	Capitalization/ spelling	124	Proper nouns/ spelling
95	Setting	110	Capitalization/ spelling	125	Spelling/acrostic poem
96	Fact or opinion	111	Nouns/spelling	126	Proper nouns/ spelling
97	Letter picking	112	Types of nouns/ spelling	127	Proper nouns/ spelling
98	Spelling	113	Nouns/spelling	128	Proper nouns/ spelling
99	Vowel pairing	114	Nouns/spelling	129	Proper nouns/ spelling
100	Spelling	115	Alphabetical order/ spelling/nouns	130	Spelling/nouns
101	Spelling	116	Nouns/spelling	131	Alphabetical order/ nouns
102	Punctuation/ spelling	117	Nouns/spelling	132	Synonyms/ pronouns
103	I or me/spelling	118	Nouns/spelling/ rhyming	133	Nouns/pronouns
104	Capital I/spelling	119	Nouns/spelling	134	Spelling review
105	Capitalization/ spelling	120	Nouns/spelling	135	Grammar review

Completion Chart for Lessons 136-180

136	Plurals with s	151	Plurals/writing	166	Compound words
137	Plurals with es	152	Plurals/pronouns	167	Word endings
138	Plurals with ies	153	Spelling/nouns	168	Word builder long o/pronouns
139	Plurals - spelling words	154	Pronouns	169	Contractions
140	Short story with plurals	155	Nouns/pronouns	170	Contractions
141	Plurals	156	Capitalization/ punctuation	171	Order and comprehension
142	Odd plurals	157	Plurals	172	Plurals
143	Odd plurals	158	Writing	173	Noun review
144	Grammar review	159	Pronouns	174	Create a character
145	Long a with silent e	160	Writing	175	Writing
146	Plurals with ves	161	Writing/pronouns	176	Comic book
147	Spelling plurals	162	Punctuation/ capitalization	177	Comic book
148	Plurals with ies	163	Word endings	178	Comic book
149	Writing sentences/ nouns	164	Spelling	179	Comic book
150	Plural rules	165	Word builder long a/pronouns	180	Comic book

Long a

Use the words in the word box to fill in the blanks below. Each word is only used once. (NOTE: the teaching lesson for this and every worksheet is located in the Parent's Guide. That separate book is necessary to make the course complete.)

made	train	base	pail	brain	pain
	fail	fade	rain	shade	

Write four words that rhyme:

_____   _____

_____   _____

_____   _____

_____   _____

Write three words that rhyme:

_____   _____

_____   _____

      _____

      _____

Write two words that rhyme:

_____   _____

_____   _____

Circle the remaining word in the word box.

Long a

Read each sentence and use a word from the word box to fill in the blank.

mail	rake	same	rain	bake

We used the _____ to get all of the leaves into a pile.

_____

I love to use my umbrella in the _____.

_____

I enjoy helping my mom _____ cupcakes.

_____

When I help with the laundry, I find two socks that are the _____.

_____

My grandma sent me a letter in the _____.

_____

Copywork

Copy this sentence onto the line below: *His wife shuddered.*

_____

Long e

Circle the long e words in the box below. Then find and circle them in the picture.

sun	sea	cloud	pole	reel	boat
reeds	bird	beak	hat	seat	
one	wheel	key	two	man	three

Long e

First, circle the words below that have the long e sound. Then write them in the blanks under the matching pictures.

tree	snake	bee	horse	leaf	bike
feet	egg	seal	pole	beach	

Copywork

Copy this sentence onto the line below: *So Jolly Robin thanked him.*

Long i

Read the story and fill in the blanks using the words below. Number the pictures in the order of the story.

bike	hide	find	slide	five	pile

I asked my brother to play a game of _____ and seek with me. I counted to _____, and then I went to _____ him. I looked behind the _____ in the garage. I rustled through the _____ of leaves. I finally found him under the _____.

☐ ☐ ☐ ☐

Long i

Sort the cupcakes! The girl wants the cupcakes with words that have a long i sound. The boy wants the rest of the cupcakes. Cut and paste the cupcakes in the right places.

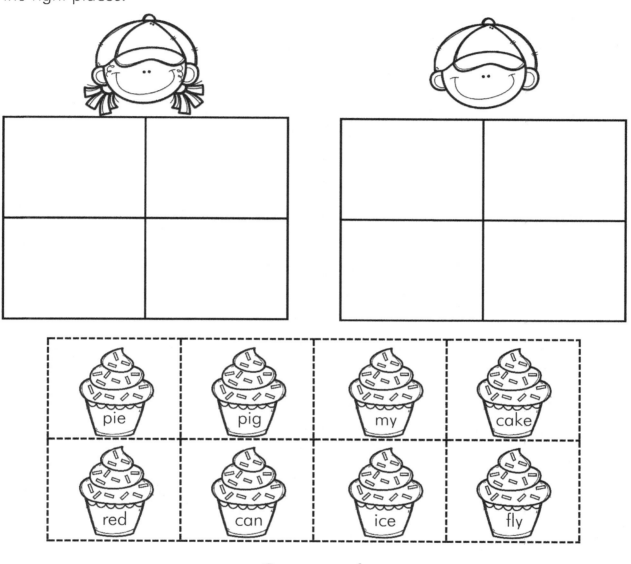

Copywork

Copy this sentence onto the lines below: *The struggle was over in a moment.*

(This page left intentionally blank)

Long o

Find and color all of the shapes with words that have the long o sound.

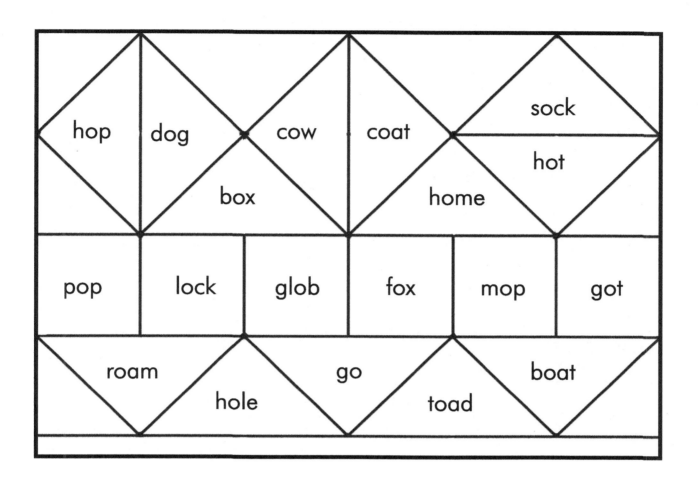

sock

hop   dog   cow   coat   hot

box   home

pop   lock   glob   fox   mop   got

roam   go   boat

hole   toad

Copywork

Copy this sentence onto the lines below: *On some days there was no sun at all.*

Long o

Read each sentence and use a word from the word box to fill in the blank.

bone	hose	snow	boat

I love to play in the _____.

My dog's favorite treat is a _____.

I watered my flowers with the _____.

I play with my toy _____ in the bathtub.

Copywork

Copy this sentence onto the lines below: *His wife, however, shook her head.*

Long u

Read the story and fill in the blanks using the words below.

clue	two	do	blue	you	glue

I made a card for my sister who turned _____. I didn't have a _____ what to make. Then my mom got out the _____ so I could make a glitter picture. I chose _____, her favorite color. I wrote the words, "Happy birthday to _____." It's fun to see all she is learning to _____.

Copywork

Copy this sentence onto the lines below: *He had expected to have a ride.*

_____

_____

_____

Long u

Let's make some stew! Color in the vegetables that have words with the long u sound in them.

Write two lines of rhyming poem using two of the long u words above.

_____

- - - - - - - - - - - - - - - - - - - -

_____

- - - - - - - - - - - - - - - - - - - -

_____

My Information

Using the lines below, print your full name, phone number and address. Write carefully and neatly.

Full name:

Phone number:

Address:

Copywork

Copy this sentence onto the lines below: *And Jolly Robin did not laugh.*

(This page left intentionally blank)

The Boy Who Cried Wolf

Cut out the following blocks and arrange them in the order they happened in the story.

The boy saw a wolf.	The father told his son to have no more drills.
The boy thought he saw the shadow of a wolf.	No one came to help.
The boy decided the villagers needed to practice a wolf drill.	The boy's father asked him to watch the sheep.

(This page left intentionally blank)

Spelling

Practice your spelling! All of these words have the same ending. Copy the word into the blank beside it. Do you know what they all mean? Draw a line from the word to the picture that matches it.

plan

can

fan

pan

van

Copywork

Copy this sentence onto the lines below: *I'd like to hear you sing.*

Spelling Word Search

Find and circle all of your spelling words from Lesson 13. Use the pictures to remind you of the words.

```
F  A  N  B  U  A  N  T  L
A  C  N  Q  D  P  A  E  S
M  R  G  A  N  L  V  A  N
U  O  H  B  C  A  P  W  A
B  E  P  D  A  N  X  Z  T
P  L  A  T  N  L  O  I  S
C  E  N  Y  U  A  F  H  A
```

Copywork

Copy this sentence onto the lines below: *And so all the weeping he might do would be merely wasted.*

_____

- -

_____

- -

_____

- -

_____

Goldilocks and the Three Bears

Cut out the following blocks and arrange them in the order they happened in the story.

The chair broke into pieces.	The three bears came home.
Goldilocks screamed and ran out of the house.	Goldilocks followed the bird into the forest.
Goldilocks tasted cobbler that was too hot.	Goldilocks fell asleep.

Copywork

Copy this sentence onto the lines below: *His cousin shook his head at that.*

_____

_____

(This page left intentionally blank)

Mystery S Picture

Color the words that end in an "s" sound blue. Color the words that end in a "z" sound green.

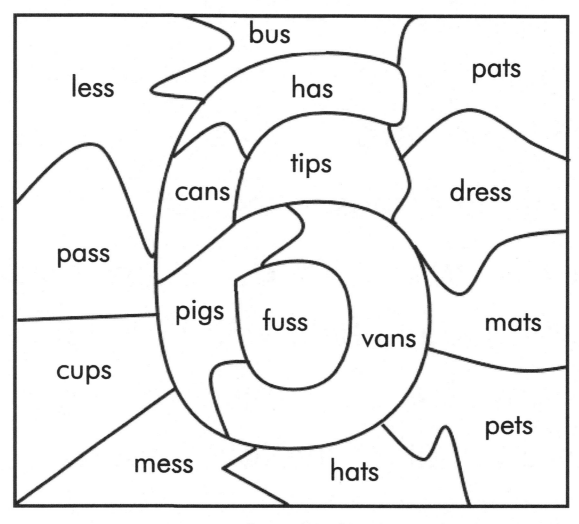

less
bus
has
pats
cans
tips
dress
pass
pigs
fuss
vans
mats
cups
mess
hats
pets

Copywork

Copy this sentence onto the lines below: *The feathered folk in Pleasant Valley were all aflutter.*

Ending Blends

Read the story and fill in the blanks using the blends in the box below.

| nt | pt | nk | nd | sk | st |

I wanted to do my mom a favor while she __sle____. First, I cleaned all of the dishes in the __si__. Next, I __we__ to __a____ my sister if she needed help with her math. It is my __be__ subject. Finally, I put away all of the toys I could __fi____. My mom was pleased!

Copywork

Copy this sentence onto the lines below: *But all the others gazed at him in amazement.*

Beginning Blends

Fill in the blanks beside each picture with its beginning blend from the box. Try to fully write at least two of the words.

ch	dr	fl	pr	sk	sl	sn	tr	str	thr

Copy this sentence onto the lines below: *Several times Jasper tried.*

Ch sound

Circle the word in each row that *begins* with the same sound as . Then write them neatly on the line.

chain

beach

basket

sheep

child

bird

_____

Circle the word in each row that *ends* with the same sound as . Then write them neatly on the line.

bench

fox

fish

cupcake

peach

pencil

_____

Copy this sentence onto the lines below: *Mr. Crow looked up quickly.*

_____

Ck sound

Circle the words that contain the "ck" sound in the box below. Then find and circle them in the picture. Finally, write them on the line.

duck	arch	lock	beach	clock	neck	art

- -

Copywork

Copy this sentence onto the lines below: *Mr. Crow was more than willing.*

- -

- -

Story Order

Read the stories and then number the pictures in the order they occurred.

The Jones family loved pets! First, they got a goldfish. Second, they got a cat. Third, they got a dog. In what order did the family get their pets?

Jamie wanted a bowl of cereal. First, she got a bowl out of the cupboard. Next, she poured the cereal in the bowl. After that, she poured in the milk. Finally, after eating her cereal she put her dishes in the sink.

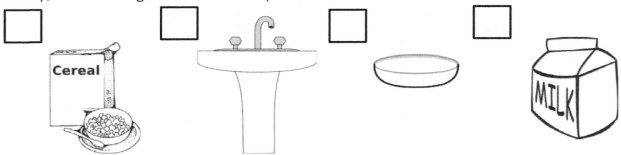

Matthew needed to finish his school work so he could play. First, he did his math work. Then, he did his reading. Next, he did his science. After that, he practiced his music. Finally, he did his computer lesson.

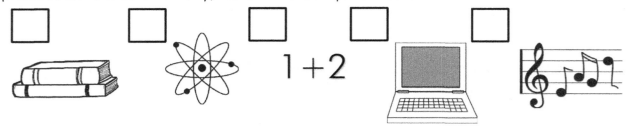

Book Report

Sit down with a parent or older sibling and tell them six things that happened in a book you just read. Have them write a sentence for each one next to the boxes below and on the next pages. Draw a picture for each sentence. Be sure to draw them in the order they happened in the story!

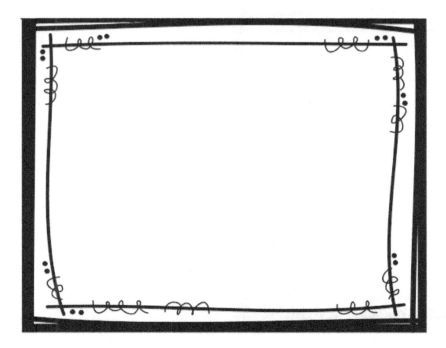

(continued on next page)

Book Report

Continue drawing your pictures in the boxes below and on the next page. Be sure to draw them in the order they happened in the story!

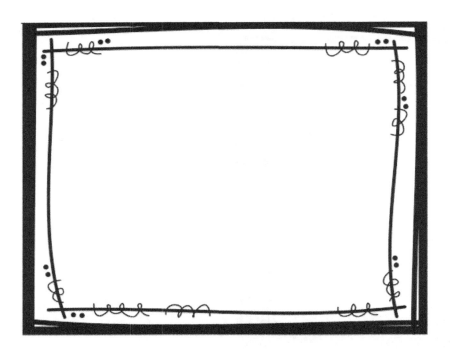

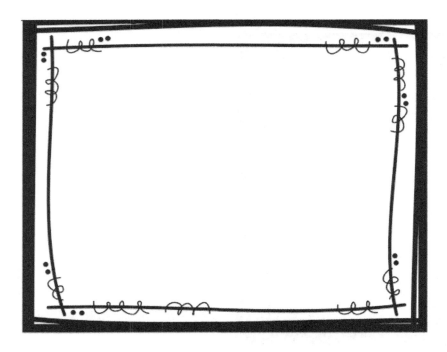

(continued on next page)

Book Report

Finish drawing your pictures in the boxes below. Be sure to draw them in the order they happened in the story!

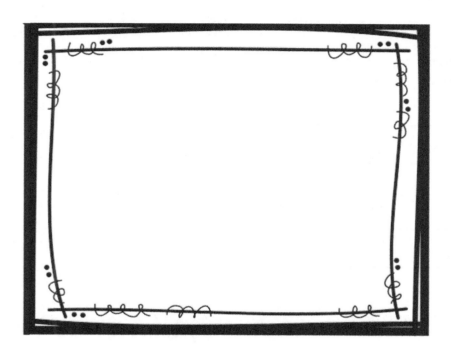

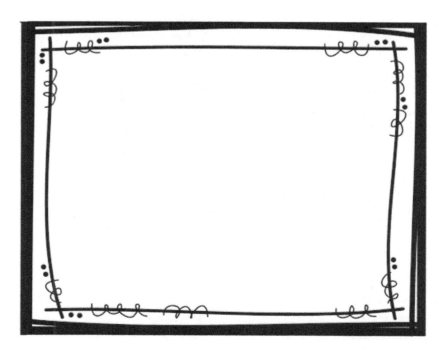

Spelling

Practice your spelling! All of these words have the same ending. Copy the word into the blank beside it. If there is not a word there, try to figure out how to spell the word that matches the picture.

cot

dot

spot

Spelling Word Search

Find and circle all of your spelling words from Lesson 23. Use the pictures to remind you of the words.

```
H  O  T  B  U  A  N  T  L
A  C  N  Q  D  Z  A  E  S
M  R  G  A  N  P  C  O  T
U  O  S  D  D  O  T  W  A
B  E  P  Z  L  T  X  Z  T
P  L  O  T  R  Z  O  I  S
C  E  T  Y  U  A  F  H  A
S  L  O  T  F  E  A  N  D
H  D  X  E  W  A  V  M  S
O  Q  R  U  L  I  W  V  U
T  Y  P  T  O  M  A  L  B
```

Ordering Sentences

Write the words in the correct order to form a proper sentence.

have   a dog.   I

_____

is Max.   name   My dog's

_____

to run.   Max   likes

_____

likes   to eat.   Max

_____

makes me   happy.   Max

_____

Ordering Sentences

Use the words in each word box to write a sentence.

| going store I mom with to my the am . |

_____

_ _

_____

_ _

_____

| wheels a you bike Can ride training without ? |

_____

_ _

_____

_ _

_____

| coming excited and birthday I'm is so My ! |

_____

_ _

_____

_____

_ _

_____

Story Writing

Write a story yourself! Choose a story you have just read or one you know well. First, you need to write the **main character** or who the story is about. Today, write down a sentence about who the story is about. Don't just write their name, write something about them. If there is another important character in the story, write about that character as well.

_____

- -

_____

- -

_____

- -

_____

- -

_____

- -

_____

- -

_____

- -

_____

- -

_____

- -

_____

- -

_____

- -

_____

Story Writing

Continue your story. Write a sentence about what the main character did in the story. Then write a sentence that tells what happened when the main character did that.

Story Writing

Finish your story. Write what happens at the end of the story. What does the main character do? Now write your last sentence. What happened when the main character did that?

Story Writing

Read aloud the story you wrote. Do you think you did a good job saying the beginning, middle and end? Draw a picture that **illustrates** or shows what happens in part of the story you wrote.

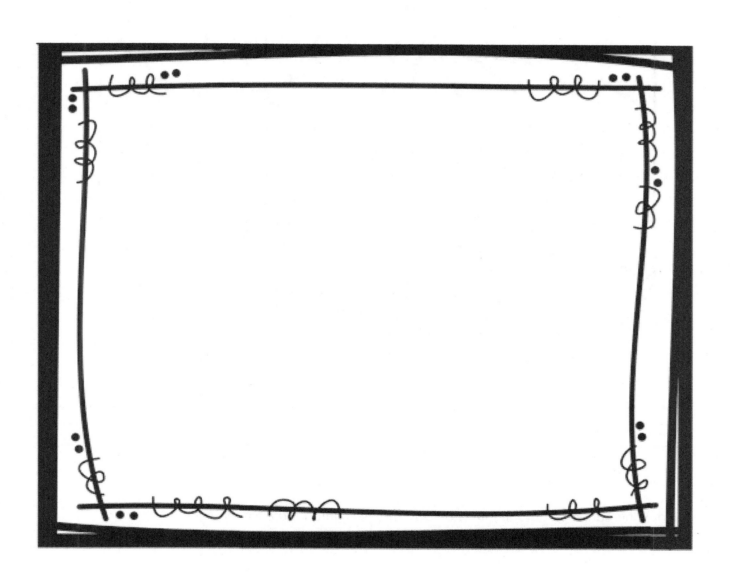

Show me the Treasure!

Color brown the words that begin with the same beginning sound in 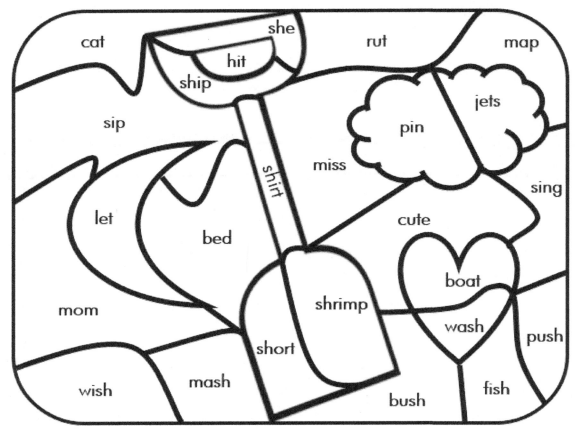. Color yellow the ones that end with the same ending sound in ⌐. Color the rest blue.

cat
she
rut
map
hit
ship
jets
sip
pin
miss
shirt
sing
let
cute
bed
boat
mom
shrimp
wash
push
short
fish
wish
mash
bush

Write two words that begin with "sh" and two words that end with "sh" on the line below.

Copywork

Copy this sentence onto the lines below: *That was unfortunate for the mice.*

Hard and soft th

The girl wants the cupcakes with words that have a hard th like the word *this*. The boy wants the cupcakes with the soft th like the word *thank*. Cut and paste the cupcakes in the right places. Then write 5 "th" words on the lines.

the   throw   there   that

myth   with   then   both

Copy this sentence onto the lines below: *It was a really good thing for Solomon Owl.*

(This page left intentionally blank)

Who Whistled?

Circle the words in the word box that begin with the same sound as . Then find those words in the puzzle below. Finally, write them on the lines.

| wheel | ship | chop | whale | shape | wheat |
| plum | whisk | draw | whistle | school | treat |

```
W  H  I  S  K  A  N  T  L
A  H  N  Q  D  Z  A  E  S
M  R  P  W  H  A  L  E  P
U  W  T  A  I  O  W  W  A
L  H  O  Z  L  T  H  Z  T
P  E  P  T  R  T  I  I  S
W  E  R  Y  U  A  S  H  A
H  L  O  H  F  E  T  N  D
E  D  X  E  W  A  L  M  S
A  Q  R  U  L  I  E  V  U
T  Y  P  T  O  M  A  L  B
```

Trigraphs

Choose the correct trigraph from the box below to make each word complete and finish the story. Then write three of the completed words on the lines.

thr   shr

My sister and I played a game of catch. I _____**ew** the ball to her.

Instead of catching it, she _____**ieked** and jumped out of the way. The ball landed in the _____**ub**. I asked her if she was going to catch the ball. She _____**ugged** and said, "I get _____**ee** strikes, right?" On my next _____**ow** she caught the ball and said, "What a _____**ill**!"

_____

_____

_____

_____

Silent e

Help the gingerbread boy get to the gingerbread house. If you come to a word with a silent e and a long vowel sound, go left ⬅. If you come to a word with a short vowel sound, go right ➡. Then write four silent e words on the lines.

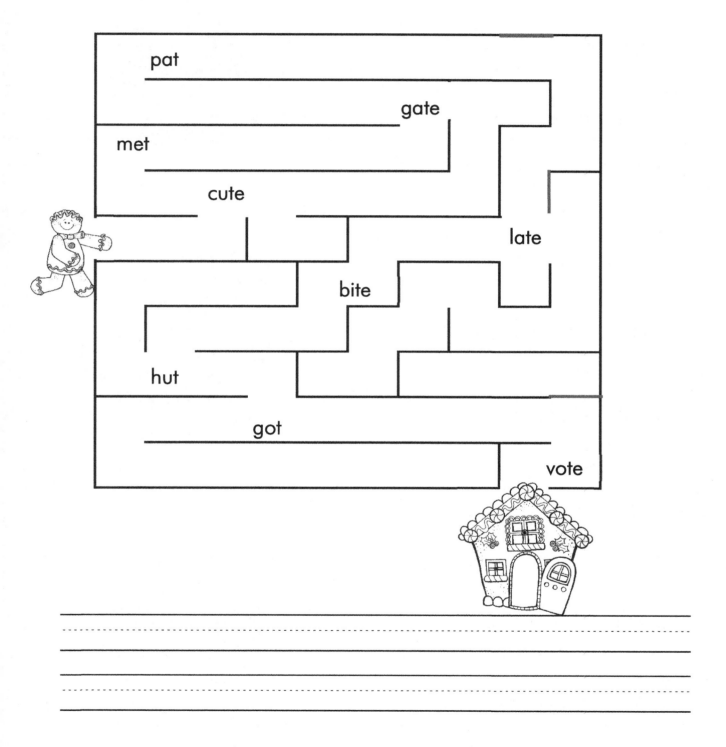

Main Idea

Circle the sentence that best describes the main idea for each picture.

The penguin is a dancer.

The penguin is an artist.

The caterpillar is friendly.

The caterpillar is mean.

The girl is afraid.

The girl is happy.

Ending Punctuation

Circle the punctuation that should go at the end of each sentence.

My mom is going to the store to buy milk

.   ?   !

Watch out for that snake

.   ?   !

What time is it

.   ?   !

I can't wait for my birthday

.   ?   !

My favorite animal at the zoo was the leopard

.   ?   !

What color is your bike

.   ?   !

Copywork

Copy this sentence onto the lines below: *Then Solomon sat up and listened.*

Capital I

Rewrite the sentences so that they are correct. Remember that the letter I is always capitalized when it is by itself as the word I.

Do you know how old i am?

_____

- -

_____

i love to go to the park.

_____

- -

_____

My friends and i like to play games.

_____

- -

_____

i love my family.

_____

- -

_____

i am special.

_____

- -

_____

Is or Are

Fill in the blanks with either **is** or **are**. Read the sentence out loud to figure out which word fits best.

Today _____ my sister's birthday.

We _____ going to the park.

The park _____ her favorite place.

We _____ having ice cream.

Her favorite flavor _____ mint.

My favorite _____ chocolate chip.

We _____ going to have fun!

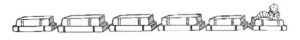

Is or Are

Fill in the blanks with either **is** or **are**. Use *is* if the sentence is about one thing.
Use *are* if the sentence is about more than one thing.

The traffic _____ heavy today.

The cars _____ moving slowly.

A bus _____ at the front.

It _____ stopping.

People _____ getting on the bus.

The vehicles _____ moving again.

Copywork

Copy this sentence onto the lines below: *"What have you been eating?" she inquired.*

_____

_____

_____

Long and Short a

Color in the spaces with words with a short a sound blue. Color in the spaces with words with a long a sound gray. What long a sound picture do you see?

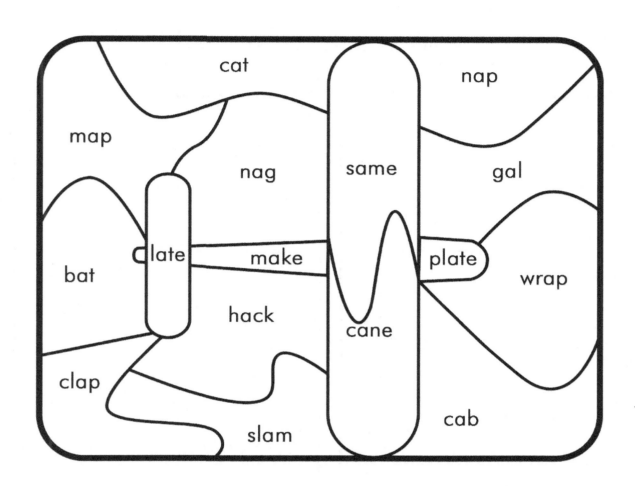

Copywork

Copy this sentence onto the lines below: *"Good!" she exclaimed with a smile.*

_____

- -

_____

- -

_____

Long and Short e

Put all the words with the short e sound in the box with the bed. Put all of the words with the long e sound in the box with the feet.

get	meal	seat	mess	sell
team	ten	bead	seek	gel

Copywork

Copy this sentence onto the lines below: *It was different with Benjamin Bat.*

Long and Short i

For each sentence, choose the word that best fits and write it on the line.

My dog _____ his toy.   bit   bite

The gum cost a _____.   dim   dime

I love to _____.   slid   slide

We have a _____ tree.   pin   pine

A bird is on the _____.   limb   lime

We already _____ a match. lit   lite

I _____ the color blue.   lick   like

(This page left intentionally blank)

Long and Short o

Sort the cupcakes! The girl wants the cupcakes with words that have a short o sound. The boy wants the cupcakes with the long o sound. Cut and paste the cupcakes.

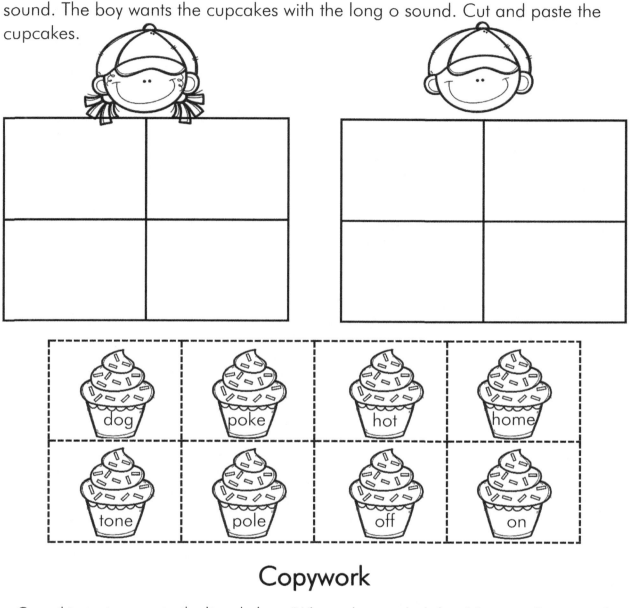

Copywork

Copy this sentence onto the lines below: *"What makes you think that?" Benjamin Bat inquired.*

(This page left intentionally blank)

Long and Short u

Put all the words with the short u sound in the box with the hut. Put all of the words with the long u sound in the box with the cube.

mutt	pup	chute	rug	tube
cute	prune	hug	duke	cup

Copywork

Copy this sentence onto the lines below: *"Oh, I shall be willing to step outside," Solomon told him.*

Inference

It is cold outside. We sang "Joy to the World" at church on Sunday. There is a big tree in my living room. Can you make an *inference* (read between the lines, make a guess based on the information you have) about what time of year it is? Draw a picture of what that time of year looks like at your house.

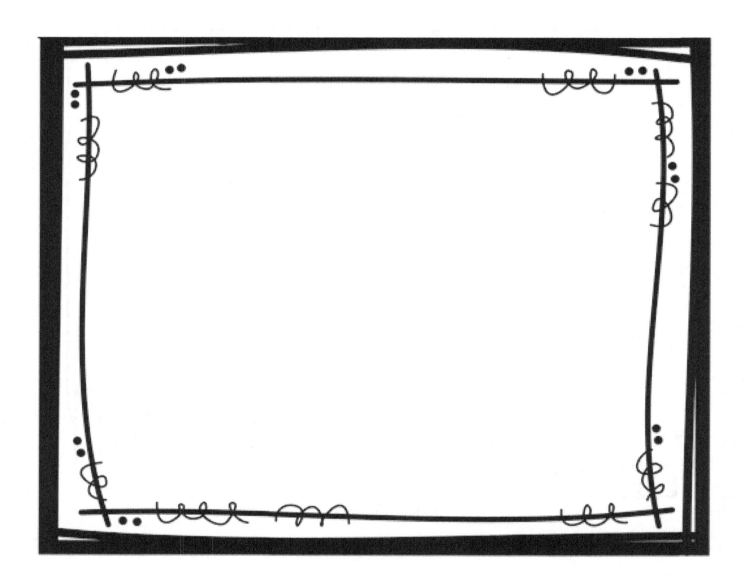

Punctuation

Fill in the punctuation mark that best fits each sentence.

I'm so scared

What is your name

My dog likes to run and play

How are you today

Stop

Watch out

My favorite subject is math

What is your favorite subject

Copywork

Copy this sentence onto the lines below: *"You surely ought to be glad to please your own cousin,"*
he told Simon.

Inference

As I was watering my carrots, I saw an adorable bunny in the yard. I quietly went inside. The next day, two of my carrots were gone. Can you make an *inference* (read between the lines, make a guess based on the information you have) about what happened to my carrots? Draw a picture below.

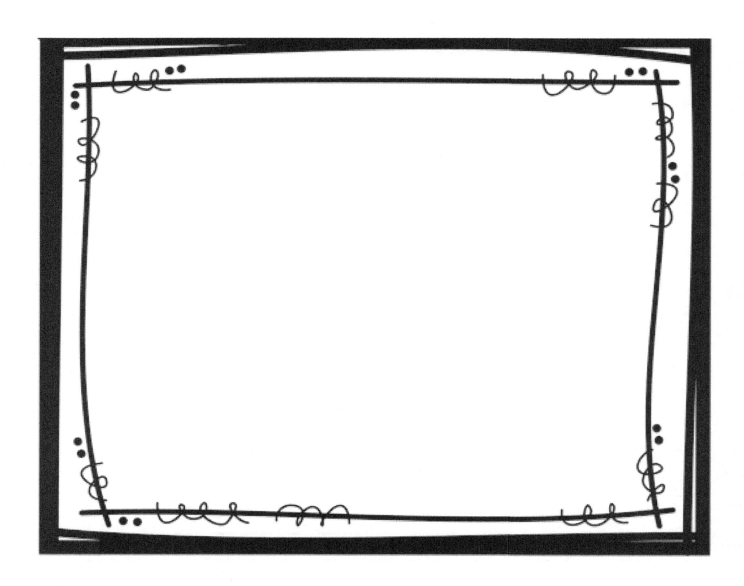

Picture Order

Put these pictures in the order they would happen. Write the number order in the boxes beside the pictures.

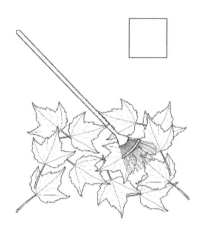 □

 □

 □

 □

 □

 □

 □

 □

 □

Inference

It's your turn. Describe a cat. Make the reader or listener make an inference. Here's an example with a dog: *I have a pet. He barks. He scratches behind his ear. He waggles when he's happy. What is he?* Try to describe a cat without actually saying it is a cat. Make your reader guess!

_____
_____
_____
_____
_____
_____
_____
_____
_____
_____
_____
_____
_____
_____
_____
_____
_____
_____

Ar Blend

These "ar" words are scrambled! Unscramble them and then find them in the puzzle below. Use the pictures for hints if you need them.

| arkb | rac | rkahs | rcta | trad | thacr |

```
C H A R T A N T L
A Z N Q D Z A E S
R C G A N M N L H
U A H C B A R K A
B R N D A R T Z R
P T A T K N O I K
C E P Y U A F H A
```

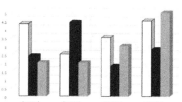

Can you think of any other "ar" words? Write them below.

_____

- -

_____

- -

_____

Blends: ir, ur, er

Fill in the blank with the proper blend from the box.

ir	ur	er

I like __t__ __key__ and gravy.

I got __th__ __d__ place in the race.

Do you like beef __j__ __ky__?

Dancers like to spin and __tw__ __l__.

The farmer __ch__ __ned__ the butter.

Or sound

Circle the words that contain the "or" sound in the box below. Then find and circle them in the picture.

| fork | barn | curl | shorts | horn | storm | art |

Make inferences! Circle the answer that best fits. Explain to someone why you chose the answer you did.

Andrew put on his pajamas.

1) It was bedtime.   2) He was cold.   3) It was morning.

Jessica dropped the mail and it swirled around the driveway.

1) It was hot.   2) It was windy.   3) It was raining.

Her hair was soft and clean.

1) She was running.   2) She was sleeping.   3) She just had a bath.

(This page left intentionally blank)

Where's My Tire?

The trucks are missing their tires! Cut and paste the tires with words that rhyme with "tire" onto the trucks. Then write "fire" and 3 words that rhyme with it.

(This page left intentionally blank)

Reader Bear

Mr. Bear only wants to read books with words that rhyme with his name. Color in the books that rhyme with "bear." Then write five words that rhyme with bear. Can you think of any new ones?

square   there   hair

soar   doctor   share

pear   floor   chair

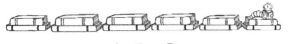

A-B-C

Do you remember your ABCs? Connect the dots in alphabetical order to reveal the picture.

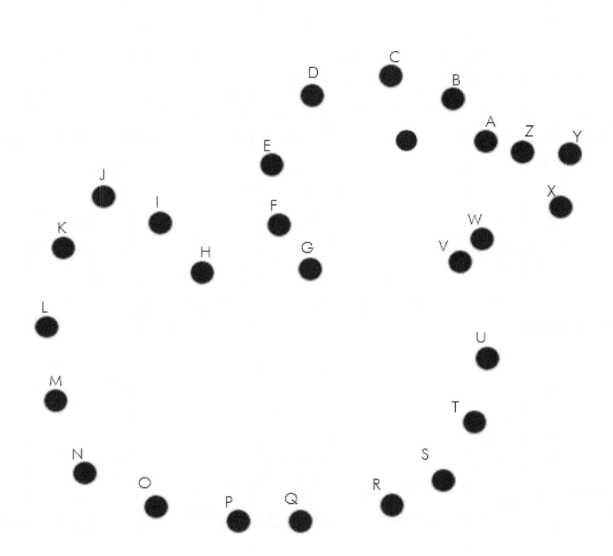

What "ck" word did you draw?

_____

- -

_____

A-B-C

Write your alphabet. Make each letter carefully and neatly. Be sure to write them in order!

A-B-C

Get the bookworm to the rest of the books! Start with the capital A in the top row and then move to the B and on through the alphabet in order. Once you get to Z, move to the lowercase a and keep continuing through the alphabet until you find the books.

X	R	L	A	B	C	L	K
Q	T	S	O	E	D	Z	Y
J	I	H	G	F	J	K	S
K	B	G	J	L	C	N	P
L	M	Q	S	U	W	Y	A
I	N	O	P	Q	T	K	Z
O	R	E	S	R	D	B	V
F	X	H	T	C	F	H	M
C	E	D	U	V	W	X	J
A	R	G	S	L	Z	Y	T
n	q	h	s	m	a	b	c
b	w	a	y	r	g	f	d
e	d	o	q	u	k	t	e
p	r	j	c	n	x	g	f
v	y	l	k	j	i	h	c
i	u	m	n	o	p	b	l
b	d	i	s	f	q	r	s
p	v	o	x	w	v	u	t
z	x	t	y	l	g	z	a
a	h	e	z	j	m	w	k

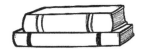

A-B-C

Circle the first letter of each word. Cut the strips out and lay the words out in alphabetical order.

 fork

- -

carrot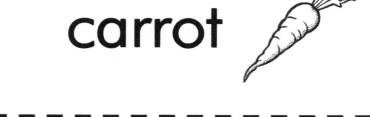

- -

egg

- -

apple

- -

 drink

- -

banana

(This page left intentionally blank)

A-B-C

Circle the first letter of each word. Cut the strips out and lay the words out in alphabetical order.

fish

 caterpillar

---

ladybug

 bow

---

sailboat

 pencil

(This page left intentionally blank)

Crazy Sentences

Pick one phrase from each box to make a crazy sentence. Write it on the lines at the bottom. Be sure to start with a capital letter and end with a period.

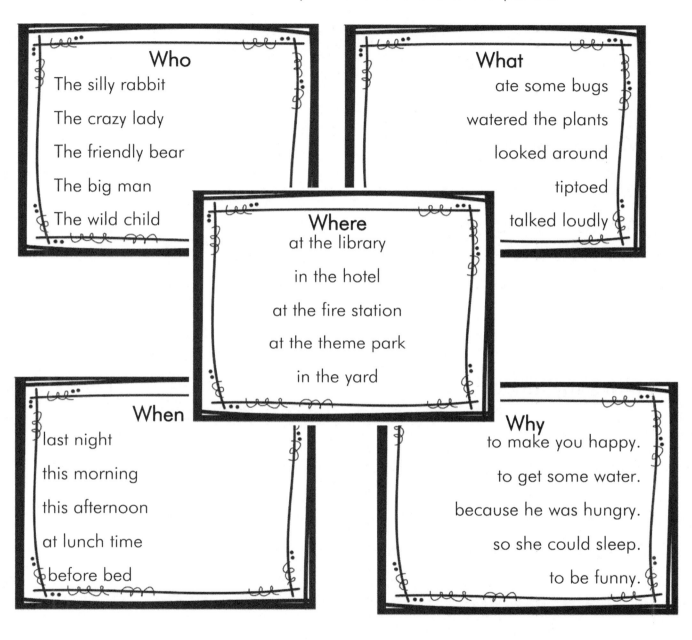

Who
The silly rabbit
The crazy lady
The friendly bear
The big man
The wild child

What
ate some bugs
watered the plants
looked around
tiptoed
talked loudly

Where
at the library
in the hotel
at the fire station
at the theme park
in the yard

When
last night
this morning
this afternoon
at lunch time
before bed

Why
to make you happy.
to get some water.
because he was hungry.
so she could sleep.
to be funny.

Punctuation

Choose the correct punctuation mark for each sentence. Circle the one that you think fits best.

My dog is my best friend   .   !   ?

May I please have a snack   .   !   ?

Where are your shoes   .   !   ?

Get down   .   !   ?

I love my family   .   !   ?

Stop   .   !   ?

What is your favorite color   .   !   ?

I have a hole in my sock   .   !   ?

Help   .   !   ?

Punctuation

Write the correct punctuation mark at the end of each sentence. Use the box to help you remember your choices.

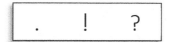

| . | ! | ? |

You'll never believe what happened today

Are you feeling okay

I enjoy helping my mom at the grocery store

Hooray

We went to the zoo and saw the elephants

Oh my

What did you have for lunch today

Where are my pants

I love doing science experiments

Correct the Sentences

Correct the sentences below. Remember that all sentences must begin with a capital letter and end with proper punctuation.

my favorite animal is a koala bear

We are going to church in the morning

have you ever traveled out of the country?

what are we having for dinner tonight

it is so hot outside!

i'm freezing

What is your name

I love pizza

Bonus tricky one:

my dad's name is Steve?

Write Your Own

Write your own sentences on the lines below. The first one should end in a period. (.) The second one should end in a question mark. (?) The third one should end in an exclamation point. (!)

Knock, Knock

Write a knock knock joke. Use a period, exclamation point, and question mark. Here is an example:

Knock, knock.
Who's there?
Ash.
Ash who?
Bless you!

Descriptive Animals

Choose an animal. Draw a picture of it in the box. Now pretend you are that animal and describe yourself. Use a period and an exclamation point. End with the question, "Who am I?" Here's an example:

I have four legs. I run faster than everyone else! Who am I?

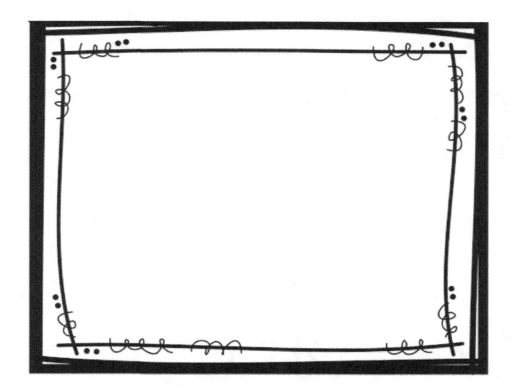

Shape Poem

Write a poem about a tree in the shape of the tree below.

Silly Boy

Write about this silly boy. Try to use a period, a question mark and an exclamation point.

Speech Practice

Read through these knock knock jokes and choose several to read aloud to someone. Use your voice to show which sentences end in a period, which end in a question mark, and which end in an exclamation point. If you're not sure how to do that, ask a parent before you begin.

Knock, knock.
Who's there?
Ash.
Ash who?
Bless you!

Knock, knock.
Who's there?
Orange.
Orange who?
Orange you thankful for Easy Peasy
All-in-One Homeschool?

Knock, knock.
Who's there?
Shower.
Shower who?
Shower is hot today!

Knock, knock.
Who's there?
Dogs go.
Dogs go who?
No, dogs go "woof"!

Knock, knock.
Who's there?
Olive.
Olive who?
Olive you!

Knock, knock.
Who's there?
Annie.
Annie who?
Annie body home?

Knock, knock.
Who's there?
Needle.
Needle who?
Needle little time to come up with
more jokes.

Knock, knock.
Who's there?
Canoe.
Canoe who?
Canoe come here for a minute?

Knock, knock.
Who's there?
Harry.
Harry who?
Harry up, it's cold out here!

Knock, knock.
Who's there?
Megan.
Megan who?
Megan end to these knock knock
jokes!

Phonics Fishing

Help the fisherman catch the fish that properly completes the word.
Circle the fish with the right beginning or ending letter.

  __ ug

 b   h   r   m

 __ ox

 b   s   f   l

 __ oy

 t 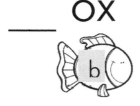 d   s  b

 bir __

 k   v   x   d

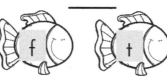 flowe __

 f t r n

 gir __

 l   d   w   h

(This page left intentionally blank)

Matching

Match the vowel sounds. Cut out the squares, mix them up and lay them face down on the table. Play a game of Memory, matching words that have the same vowel sound (they may be spelled differently).

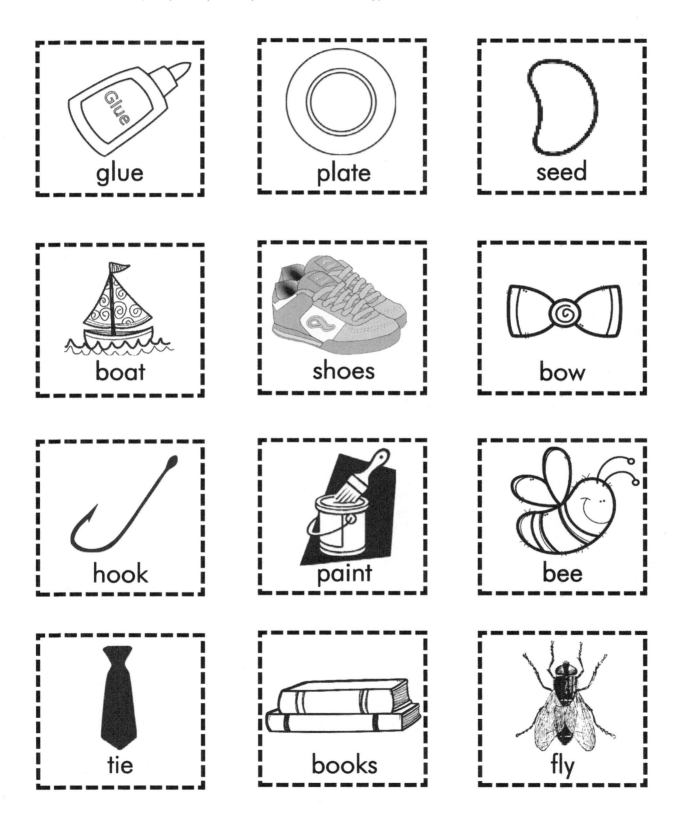

glue

plate

seed

boat

shoes

bow

hook

paint

bee

tie

books

fly

(This page left intentionally blank)

Make a Cartoon

Draw a picture and then add some text to make your own cartoon!

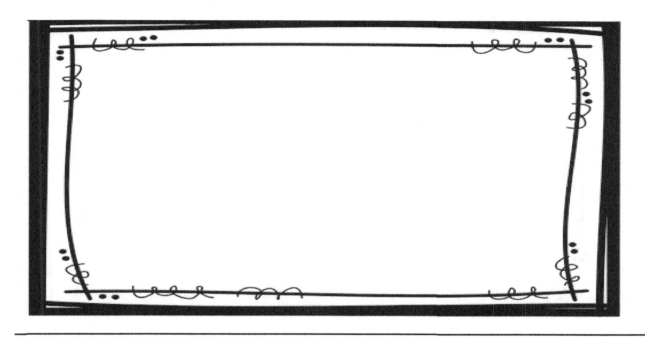

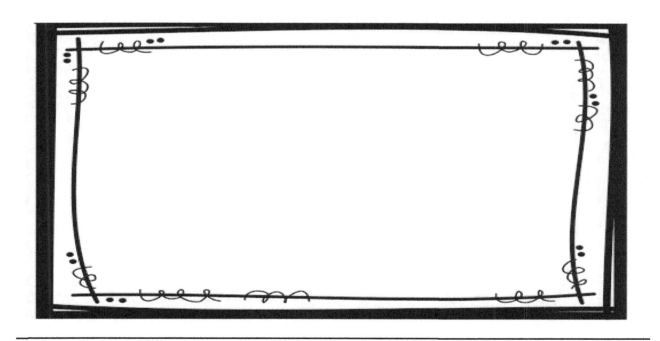

Make a Cartoon

Draw a picture and then add some text to make your own cartoon!

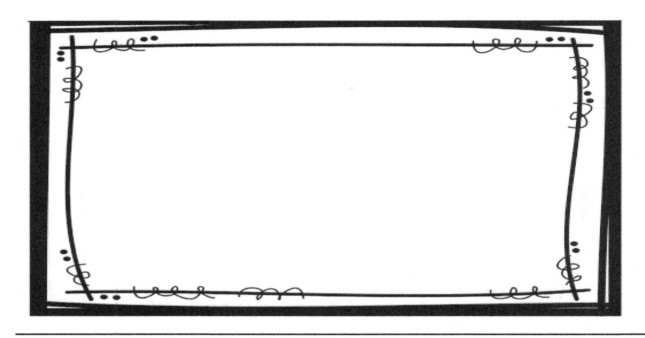

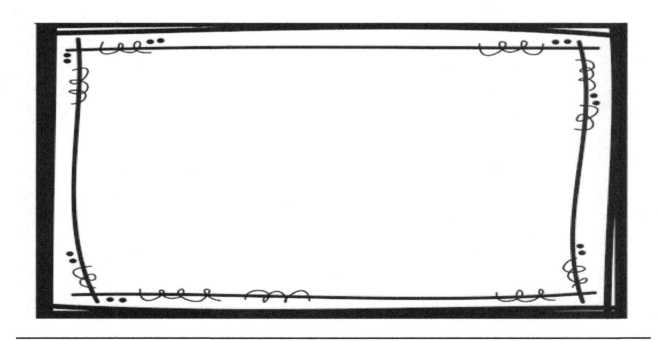

Make a Cartoon

Draw a picture and then add some text to make your own cartoon!

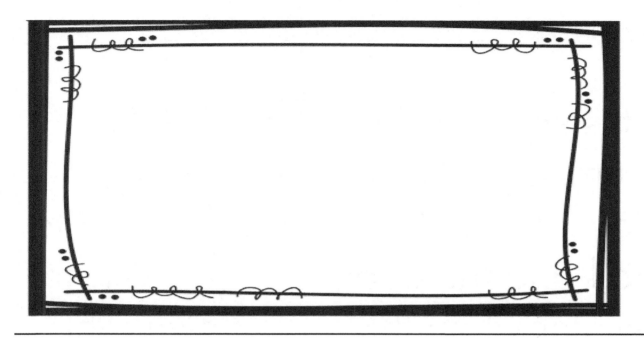

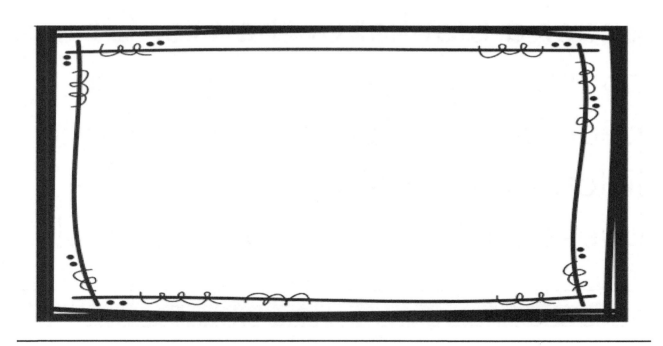

Weather Words

Fill in the blanks using the words in the word box. Pay attention to the clues you get in the sentences to decide which word goes in the blank. Then describe your favorite season.

| drizzle | freezing | humid | crisp |

It is so hot and _____ this summer! I know some people love it, but I'm looking forward to fall and the cool, _____ air. In winter when the air is downright _____, I love to snuggle up under a blanket by the fire. Of course, during the spring it's so peaceful to open my window and listen to the falling _____. I guess each season has its perks!

_____

_____

_____

My Favorite Room

Use this brainstorming page to describe your favorite room. Start by filling in the main idea blank, then fill in the boxes below.

Main idea:

My favorite room is _____

Looks like	Sounds like	Smells like

Tastes like	Feels like	Makes me feel

My Favorite Room

Use your brainstorming page from lesson 77 to write about your favorite room. Start with your main idea, then write one sentence from each of the top three boxes. Here is an example: **My favorite room is the kitchen. It is big and has lots of room for the whole family. In the kitchen, I hear pigeons cooing out the window all the time. It often smells of boiling soup.**

My Favorite Room

Use your brainstorming page from lesson 77 to continue to write about your favorite room. Today, write one sentence from each of the bottom three boxes. Here is an example: In the kitchen, I taste the soup to see if it needs more salt. It is the coolest room in the house when the wind blows through the window. The kitchen makes me feel happy, as long as it is clean!

My Favorite Room

Draw a picture of your favorite room. Read what you wrote on Lessons 78 and 79 to a sibling or parent. Be sure to speak clearly and loudly. Show them your picture. Ask them to describe their favorite room to you.

What Happened?

Write a silly story about this picture. How did this happen?

My Family

Describe your family.

My Favorite Thing

What's your favorite thing to do? Why do you like to do it? Describe it below.

What I Had For Dinner

What did you have for dinner yesterday? Include colors and smells!

What Happened?

Write a silly story about these pictures. Why was the ladybug sad? What happened to make it happy again?

Copywork

Copy this sentence: *Jolly Robin's worrying wife wouldn't give him a moment's peace.*

_____

_____

_____

_____

That sentence said "worrying wife." Both words started with a W. Can you think of another pair of words that start with the same letter? For example: **Jolly Robin's sad son.**

_____

Now write a new sentence using the words you chose. For example: **Jolly Robin's sad son said he wanted to play.**

_____

_____

_____

Copywork

Copy this sentence: *Jolly Robin told his wife how he swooped down over Reddy Woodpecker's head.*

Picture Jolly Robin flying over Reddy Woodpecker. Now picture him swooping down over him. Which is more exciting? Can you write an exciting sentence?

Punctuation

Choose the proper way to write each sentence.

a. Jim has a dog   b. jim has a dog?   c. Jim has a dog.   d. Jim has a dog?

a. Pat is a girl.   b. pat is a girl?   c. Pat is a girl?   d. pat is a girl.

a. joey is sad?   b. Joey is sad   c. Joey is sad.   d. Joey is sad?

a. Is Debra mad.   b. is Debra mad?   c. Is Debra mad   d. Is Debra mad?

a. are you okay.   b. Are you okay?   c. are you okay?   d. Are you okay.

a. Sue is here.   b. sue is here.   c. Sue is here?   d. Sue is here

a. She is napping   b. she is napping?   c. She is napping.   d. she is napping

a. Drew is gone.   b. Drew is gone   c. drew is gone?   d. drew is gone

Copywork

Copy this sentence: *One day Reddy Woodpecker was tap, tap, tapping on a tall poplar that grew beside the brook.*

"Tap" is a word that sounds like its name. Can you think of other words that sound like their name? Buzz, pop, swish. What are some others? Can you write a sentence using a sound word?

Sound Words

Here are some more sound words. For each one, read it out loud and say it like the sound it's naming.

achoo!

tick tock

choo choo

moo

baa

There are lots of other words that make the sound of their name. Can you think of another one? Write it in a sentence below.

_____

_____

_____

_____

_____

Setting

Think about a book you are reading. Draw a picture of where the main character lives or where the story takes place. Draw what you imagine it looks like. This is called the story's **setting**.

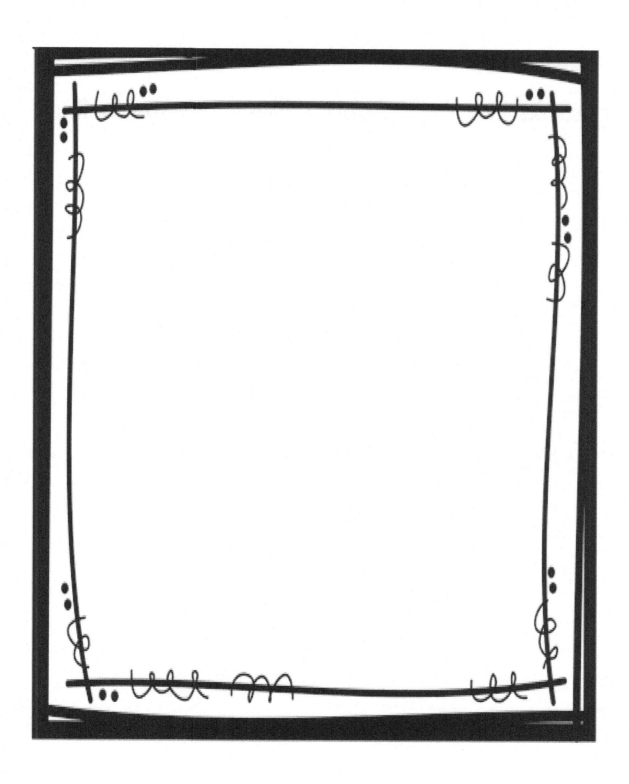

Describing the Setting

Think about your book again. Write description words about where the main character lives or where the story takes place. Fill in the boxes below with words that tell what you would see, feel, hear, smell, and taste if you were where the story takes place.

Looks like	Sounds like	Smells like

Tastes like	Feels like	Makes me feel

Describing the Setting

Use your worksheet from Lesson 92. Write a description of where the main character lives. Write sentences using all of the words you wrote in the senses boxes.

_____

- -

_____

- -

_____

- -

_____

- -

_____

- -

_____

- -

_____

- -

_____

- -

_____

- -

_____

- -

_____

- -

_____

- -

Describing the Setting

Read your description of where the main character lives to someone. Ask them to draw a picture of it below. Does it look like you imagined?

Revise Your Description

If the other person's picture doesn't look right, what could you add to your description to help them draw a better picture? This is called **revising** or fixing up what you wrote. Every writer, even professional ones, revise their work. They go back and fix problems and make it better.

_____

_____

_____

_____

_____

_____

_____

_____

_____

_____

_____

_____

_____

Fact or Opinion?

Choose if the following statements are facts or opinions. Facts are things that are true for everyone — you can show that they are true. Opinions are things you cannot show are true. They differ from person to person.

The girl is wearing a hat.

fact   opinion

The boy has a goofy grin.

fact   opinion

There are three cherries.

fact   opinion

The butterfly is pretty.

fact   opinion

The apple looks delicious.

fact   opinion

Letter Picking

Pick the cherry that has the correct ending to properly spell the word.

bo___

mi___

we___

be___

se___

smo___

ca___

ri___

ti___

to___

Copywork

Copy this sentence onto the lines below: *Reddy Woodpecker had no patience with him.*

Spelling

Look at the picture and listen to the word as it's read. Spell it on the line.

_____

_____

_____

_____

_____

_____

Copywork

Copy this sentence onto the lines below: *It's no wonder Reddy was angry.*

_____

_____

_____

Vowel Pairing

Use the apples to pick the vowels that are missing from each word.

sq___rrel
ui oa ea ee

b___t
oi oa ui ie

w___k
oa ui ee ie

bab___s
oi ie ea oa

s___t
ui oi ee oa

pl___n
ie ee oa ai

sp___n
oo ee ie ai

r___d
ea ui oo ie

t___s
oo ui oe ai

___nk
ea oi ai ui

Copywork

Copy this sentence onto the lines below: *Then Frisky sat on a limb and glared at him.*

_____

- -

_____

_____

- -

_____

Spelling

Unscramble the letters to spell the words that match the pictures.

d i b r   _____

t b a o   _____

e f t e   _____

a l e s   _____

Copywork

Copy this sentence onto the lines below: *Frisky did not intend to go hungry when winter came.*

_____

_____

_____

Spelling

Use the lines below to write your spelling words as they are read to you from the Parent's Guide.

Punctuation

Fill in the punctuation mark that best fits each sentence.

I'm so excited

When is your birthday

My sister loves to sing

I enjoy dancing

Help

What is your favorite food

How old are you

Spelling

Fill in the missing letter.

g__rl

i u e o

f__om

l r y a

pr__y

o i a u

h__nt

a o u e

cav__

u l e r

do__n

e z a w

I or Me

Fill in the blank with **I** or **me** to make the sentence correct.

_____ just baked my first cake.

Come with _____ to the kitchen.

_____ will show you my cake.

You can tell _____ what you think.

_____ think it looks delicious.

Will you eat it with _____?

Spelling

Play a game of hangman. Cross off the letters as you guess them to keep track.

a b c d e f g h i j k l m n o p q r s t u v w x y z

— — — — —

Capital I

Rewrite the sentences so that they are correct. Then practice your spelling by finding the words from the box in the puzzle at the bottom of the page.

i love spaghetti.

_____

- -

_____

Do you think i am smart?

_____

- -

_____

i always try my best.

_____

- -

_____

May i go first?

_____

- -

_____

```
F  A  P  A  R  T  P  T  L
I  C  N  Q  D  Z  I  R  P
L  R  G  I  F  T  N  Y  U
L  W  H  I  P  A  E  P  R
B  I  N  D  E  N  X  Z  X
P  C  A  L  L  T  A  R  S
```

| fill | gift | whip | pine | try | call | trap |

Capitalization

Underline the words in each sentence that need to be capitalized. Remember that all names are capitalized – names of people, places, days, months, etc. Also remember that each sentence should start with a capital letter. Then use the lines at the bottom to write your spelling words as they're read to you from the Parent's Guide.

the children were excited for their trip to the zoo on friday.

mr. smith brought the ham for our easter meal.

the fire station is on main street.

mary's favorite holiday is christmas.

in july we see a lot of fireworks.

Spelling

Use the lines below to write your spelling words as they are read to you from the Parent's Guide.

Copywork

Copy this sentence onto the line below (pay attention to the punctuation): *No, it wasn't that.*

(continued on next page)

Blending Words

Cut out the strips, and then match up the beginning sounds with the ending sounds to make different words. Read them out loud. The sounds with a dot on the left of the boxes are beginning sounds, the sounds with a dot on the right of the boxes are ending sounds. Each word should begin and end with a dot. How many words can you make? Are they real words?

● bl	● p	ock ●
● cl	● h	ub ●
● sh	● sp	at ●
● r	● spl	ack ●
● s	● b	est ●
● t	● n	ot ●
● shr	● ch	an ●

(This page left intentionally blank)

Missing Letter

Fill in the missing letter from each spelling word.

ag___in   a___y

a e i u   c r n l

ba___y   be___t

s b r d   v t d a

blo___k   a___m   bak___

c t s e   k p h r   c s y e

bo___e   bl___e   br___g

s n l t   a i o u   e o u a

Copywork

Copy this sentence onto the lines below: *Old Mr. Toad just laughed.*

Spelling Word Search

Find the words in the puzzle below.

```
B L U E D B N B V A M G G H J
W Z K Y G E A A O S A N Y N O
S E C I L A L B Q K B I R T H
B E N T Y T A Y B E L F Z K I
B I M B E S T K R I B F B G A
L R S C N C S E I B E Z R F B
O B A G A I N G N Z L J A L O
C B A K E M R N G N T C G J N
K G T B K P U A R M L M E L E
```

again	baby	bent	blue
any	bake	best	bone
arm	beat	birth	brag
ask	belt	block	bring

Copywork

Copy this sentence onto the lines below: *By and by he turned his head.*

_____

- -

_____

- -

_____

Capitalization

Underline the words in each sentence that need to be capitalized. Remember that all names are capitalized – names of people, places, days, months, etc. Also remember that each sentence should start with a capital letter.

the campbell kids were playing in their tennessee yard.

mrs. blane went to the grocery store.

i live in the united states of america.

what is your favorite month?

my birthday is on a saturday this year.

Spelling

Play a game of hangman. Cross off the letters as you guess them to keep track.

a b c d e f g h i j k l m n o p q r s t u v w x y z

__ __ __ __ __ __ __ __ __ __

Capitalization

Underline the words in each sentence that should be capitalized. Add punctuation to the end of each sentence. Then write your spelling words as they're read to you from the Parent's Guide.

did you see james kick that ball

mary is screaming for help

you and i should meet for lunch on friday

Copywork

Copy this sentence onto the line below: *"Next time I'll get him!"*

Fishing for Nouns

A **noun** is a person, place or thing. Jeffrey, post office, ball — those are all nouns. Circle the fish below that contain nouns.

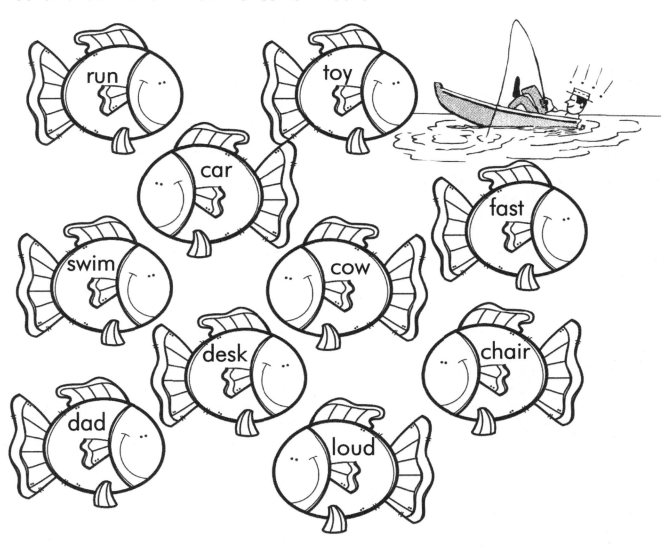

Copywork

Copy these words onto the lines below: *ship shop shape shine shirt shoe*

Different Nouns

A **noun** is a person, place or thing. There are different types of nouns. Copy the word into the blanks as you learn about nouns.

Common nouns:

girl

church

Proper nouns: name a *specific* person, place or thing

Carol

Calvary

Collective nouns: name a *group* of people, places or things

family

congregation

Fill in the missing "sh" to complete the spelling words below.

___ape   ___ine   ___ip

___irt   ___op

Copy this sentence onto the line below: *"That's good," said she.*

Sh words

Find the "sh" words in the puzzle below. Circle the ones that are nouns.

ship	shoe	shine	shape	shirt	shop

S	H	I	R	T	R	D	S	H
R	Y	S	S	W	S	T	H	L
M	G	Z	H	E	H	U	I	P
X	P	S	O	I	A	V	N	R
Z	V	H	P	R	P	I	E	X
Z	L	I	Y	X	E	E	P	S
G	W	P	G	D	M	B	N	L
B	S	H	O	E	G	Z	W	H

Circle the nouns below.

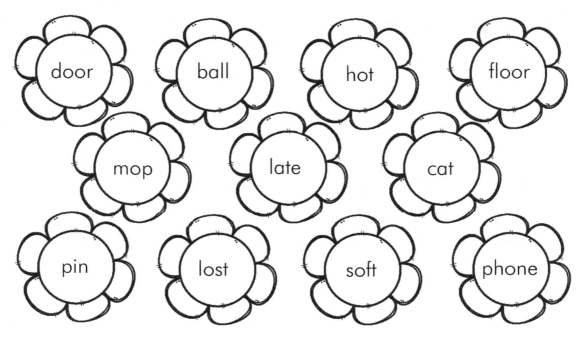

door   ball   hot   floor

mop   late   cat

pin   lost   soft   phone

Sh words

Complete the crossword puzzle using the clues below.

Across:
1. a big boat
2. can have long or short sleeves
3. a square is an example
4. you wear it over your sock

Down:
1. the sun can do this
3. what you do when you need to buy something

Underline the nouns in the sentences below:

There is wind blowing the trees.

A big bus drove through the streets.

A spider crawled across the deck.

The baseball crashed through the window.

Spelling

Write your spelling words as they are read to you. These are the words from your lesson 111 copywork.

_____   _____

_____   _____

_____   _____

_____   _____

Alphabetical Order

Put these words in alphabetical order on the lines below. Circle the nouns.

| cage | tree | food | eat | milk | drive | bank | pretty | apple | win |

1 _____   6 _____

2 _____   7 _____

3 _____   8 _____

4 _____   9 _____

5 _____   10 _____

Noun Hunt

Go around your house and find as many nouns as you can. Pick your favorites and draw them here.

Copywork

Copy these words onto the lines below: *chin chip chop cheap church churn*

_____

- -

_____

- -

_____

Noun Hunt

Underline all of the nouns in this sentence.

His big eyes filled with tears as he looked at Danny

Meadow Mouse for Danny was all torn and hurt by

the cruel claws of Hooty the Owl, and you know Peter

has a very tender heart.

Fill in the missing ch from the words below.

_____in

_____ip

_____op

_____eap

_____urch

_____urn

Rhyming Words

Think of two rhyming words. Write them here:

_____   _____
-     -
_____   _____

Read this out loud: *My ears are long. My legs are strong.* Put your two rhyming words together in short sentences like that. Read them out loud.

_____
- -
_____
- -
_____

Spelling Word Search

Find the "ch" words in the puzzle below.

chin	chip	chop	cheap	church	churn

```
C  H  I  N  T  R  D  C  H
R  Y  L  S  W  W  T  H  L
C  G  C  H  U  R  N  E  P
H  P  C  O  P  Y  V  A  R
U  V  H  H  R  R  I  P  X
R  S  I  Y  X  Q  N  P  S
C  W  P  G  D  C  H  O  P
H  P  N  B  B  G  Z  W  H
```

Ch Words

Unscramble your spelling words. Do you remember what two letters they all started with?

c n i h

_____

p h i c

_____

h o p c

_____

e c p a h

_____

h h c r u c

_____

n u r h c

_____

Copywork

Copy this sentence onto the lines below: *So Peter hurried over to the nearest tree.*

_____

_____

What are the two nouns from your copywork sentence?

_____   _____

Spelling

Write your spelling words as they are read to you. These are the words from your lesson 116 copywork.

_____   _____
------------------------------   ------------------------------
_____   _____

_____   _____
------------------------------   ------------------------------
_____   _____

_____   _____
------------------------------   ------------------------------
_____   _____

A tisket, a tasket, a noun in a basket. Circle the baskets that contain the nouns.

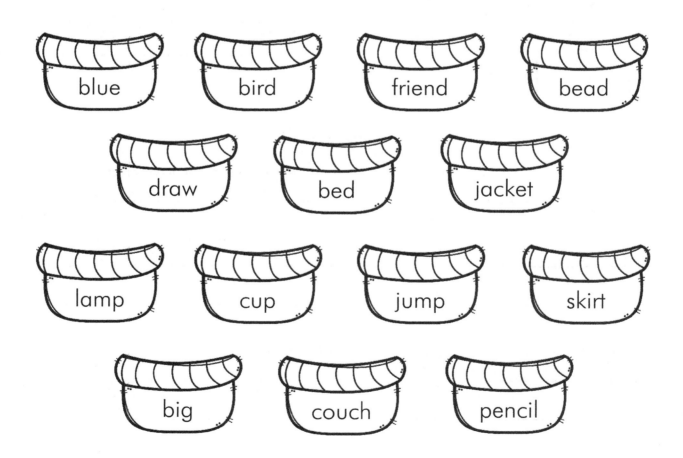

Find the Nouns

Underline the nouns in the following sentences.

Mary took the letter to the post office.

Jennifer went to the movie theater with her friends.

Michael sat on the swing next to his cousin.

David ate the apple at the table.

Charlie put tomatoes on his salad.

Jamie took her sister to the zoo.

Jason got mustard on his shirt.

Copywork

Copy these words onto the lines below: *who what why where when which*

- -

- -

Proper Nouns

Proper nouns are names of people, places, or things. Underline the proper nouns in the following sentences.

Mr. Davis went to Pittsburgh last Sunday.

My brother, Stephen, works at McDonald's.

Rachel took a jog in Central Park.

Clara went to school at Lincoln Elementary.

Natalie's birthday is Saturday.

Fill in the missing wh from the words below.

_____o

_____en

_____at

_____ere

_____y

_____ich

Wh Words

Find the "wh" words in the puzzle below.

who	what	why	when	where	which

```
W  H  E  R  E  H  A  Y  H
A  S  E  I  E  W  H  O  L
Y  S  D  R  W  A  T  R  P
O  A  C  W  H  B  W  Z  R
W  H  V  H  E  N  O  W  X
H  K  Z  A  N  L  X  A  S
Y  L  Y  T  W  K  A  B  C
V  W  H  I  C  H  T  F  H
```

Circle the proper noun and underline the common noun in this sentence:

By and by, happening to look across the snow-covered Green Meadows,

he saw something that made his heart jump.

Write words that you could use to describe a meadow. In this sentence he called it "the snow-covered Green Meadows." You could say the flat meadows, the sweet-smelling meadows. What can you think of?

_____

- -

_____

_____

- -

_____

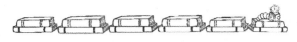

Wh Words

Unscramble your spelling words. Do you remember what two letters they all started with?

h w o

h t a w

y w h

e h w n

r e w e h

h i w h c

_____

_____

_____

_____

_____

_____

Copywork

Copy this sentence onto the lines below: *Peter Rabbit sat in his secretest place in the dear Old Briar-patch.*

_____

_____

Circle the proper nouns and underline the common nouns in the sentence you copied.

Spelling

Write your spelling words as they are read to you. These are the words from your lesson 121 copywork.

_____   _____
- - - - - - - - - - - - - - - - - -   - - - - - - - - - - - - - - - - - -
_____   _____

_____   _____
- - - - - - - - - - - - - - - - - -   - - - - - - - - - - - - - - - - - -
_____   _____

_____   _____
- - - - - - - - - - - - - - - - - -   - - - - - - - - - - - - - - - - - -
_____   _____

Acrostic Poem

An **acrostic poem** is a poem that uses the letters in a topic word to begin each line. Each line relates to or describes the topic word. For instance, if your topic word was "Mom," the first line would start with M, the second with O and the third with M. Each line would describe Mom. Write an acrostic poem below.

Find the Proper Nouns

Underline the proper nouns in the following sentences.

The Empire State Building is really tall.

Jenn got a purple hat on Wednesday.

Tim used his telescope to see Jupiter.

April is such a rainy month.

The Grand Canyon is in Arizona.

Amy lives on the corner of Lake Avenue and Elm Street.

Avery lives in California.

Copywork

Copy these words onto the lines below: *this that they thing think there*

Th Words

Fill in the missing th from the words below.

__is

__ing

__at

__ink

__ey

__ere

Can you think of six proper nouns? Remember to capitalize them!

Th Words

Find the "th" words in the puzzle below.

| this | that | they | thing | think | there |

```
T  H  E  R  E  T  F  Y  H
R  H  G  F  I  H  D  F  T
S  K  L  P  J  I  K  R  H
Z  M  Q  N  H  S  U  Z  E
T  H  A  T  G  Z  F  W  Y
P  T  H  T  H  I  N  K  S
T  H  Y  R  B  E  L  B  C
V  T  H  I  N  G  T  F  H
```

List all the proper nouns you can think of. Some examples are: the names of everyone in your family, the place you live, the name of your church, the name of some local schools.

_____

_____

_____

_____

_____

_____

Th Words

Unscramble your spelling words. Do you remember what two letters they all started with?

s t h i

t t a h

y t e h

g t n i h

k t n i h

e t r h e

_____

_____

_____

_____

_____

_____

Circle the nouns below. Put a line under the proper nouns below.

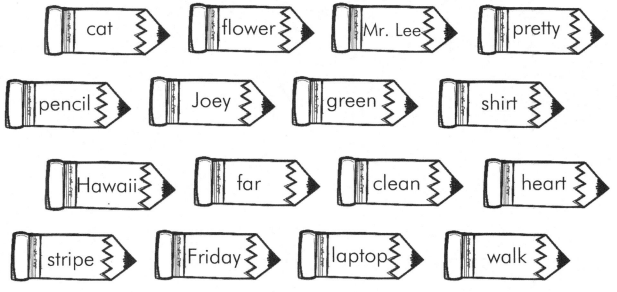

cat   flower   Mr. Lee   pretty

pencil   Joey   green   shirt

Hawaii   far   clean   heart

stripe   Friday   laptop   walk

Spelling

Write your spelling words as they are read to you. These are the words from your lesson 126 copywork.

Circle the common nouns below. Put a line under the proper nouns below.

circle   tree   frost   look

kick   Peter   flag

Cape Cod   find   hard   Monday

Write two proper nouns below. What do they need to start with?

Alphabetical Order

Put these words in alphabetical order on the lines below. Circle the nouns.

| bear | jump | sweet | film | zebra | run | yak | oar | good | police |

1 _____   6 _____

2 _____   7 _____

3 _____   8 _____

4 _____   9 _____

5 _____   10 _____

Circle the common nouns below. Put a line under the proper nouns below.

mad   cloud   Emily   friend

baby   lips   over

van   France   take   quickly

Synonyms

Synonyms are words that mean the same thing. *Start* and *begin* are synonyms. Circle the train car that is a synonym for the train engine.

A **pronoun** is a word that takes the place of a noun. Circle the best pronoun for the word indicated in each sentence.

Mary went to the store and _____ bought some ice cream. (Mary)

       she   it   they

On the way home, _____ melted a little. (the ice cream)

       she   it   they

Mary put it in the freezer for an hour when _____ got home. (Mary)

       she   it   they

Mary called her sister and _____ ate it all up. (Mary and her sister)

       she   it   they

Fishing for Nouns

Color red the fish below that contain common nouns. Color blue the fish that contain pronouns.

Spelling Word Search

Find the spelling review words in the puzzle below.

```
C K T H S H I R T W B V N O T
H X P Q W C Z A I H Y N A X H
I D R O P U H K I O S C T T I
P G K I G M N F J Q Y C Y O N
F C L T Q O T Y A U H B I B K
Z H P W H I C H B P Y A K N S
U E E T B U F P M L K F N E H
O A X R F O R T H E R E T W Q
W P F U M R L E L N Q W H S R
X J S H A P E N M U Q K D A W
O R Z F N T C M U I U Z J O L
```

think	there	chip	which	who
shape	cheap	shirt		

Copywork

Copy these words onto the lines below: *this thing where why shop shoe chop church*

Grammar Review

Answer the questions below by filling in the square beside your choice.

Which of these words comes first in alphabetical order?

☐ cake ☐ fish ☐ tree ☐ paint

Which of these letters are in alphabetical order?

☐ BCFDEG ☐ ZYXWVU ☐ JKLMNO ☐ HIJGLK

Which of these words does NOT rhyme with pie?

☐ cry ☐ lie ☐ try ☐ field

Which of these words does NOT rhyme with Tim?

☐ slim ☐ trim ☐ time ☐ limb

Which of these is a correct sentence?

☐ two hands and two feet ☐ You have two hands and two feet

☐ you have two hands and two feet ☐ You have two hands and two feet.

Which word in this sentence is a noun? My house is big.

☐ is ☐ my ☐ big ☐ house

Which word in this sentence is a proper noun? My grandparents live in Philadelphia.

☐ my ☐ Philadelphia ☐ grandparents ☐ live

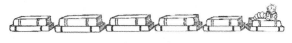

Plurals

A **plural** word is a word that means more than one. For instance, you have one bike, but two bike**s**. You add an S on to the end to make it plural. Add an S to these words to make them plural.

ball____   home____

bed____   house____

brother____   school____

door____   sister____

girl____   tree____

flower____   pool____

Copywork

Copy these plural words onto the lines below: *bikes stores cars tables friends times*

_____
- -
_____
_____
- -
_____

Plurals

Sometimes a word needs an ES on the end to make it plural. That happens when a word ends with X, SS, SH or CH. Pay attention to the words below and add either an S or an ES to make the word plural.

bucket___ bush___

church___ pencil___

brush___ torch___

princess___ prince___

fox___ flute___

dog___ cat___

Copywork

Copy these plural words onto the lines below: *washes misses brushes peaches wishes taxes*

_____

_____

_____

Plurals

When a word ends in Y, plurals can be tricky. When there is a vowel before the Y, add an S to make it plural. If there is NOT a vowel before the Y, you change the Y to an I and add ES. Make the following words plural. (When there is not a vowel before the Y, put an X on the Y and then write IES in the blank.)

baby_____   ray_____

lady_____   fly_____

monkey_____   boy_____

city_____   valley_____

family_____   tray_____

tally_____   trolley_____

Copywork

Copy these plural words onto the lines below: *toys ways days plays keys*

Plurals

Make the following words plural.

bike____

store____

friend____

miss____

peach____

try____

play____

brush____

wash____

baby____

day____

time____

tax____

way____

table____

wish____

Circle the pronouns below.

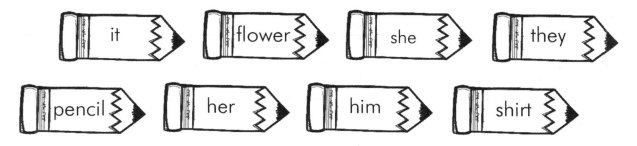

it   flower   she   they

pencil   her   him   shirt

Story Writing

Write a short story using a word from each of the copywork lists from this week. You can use your worksheet from lesson 139 for a master list of words.

_____

- -

_____

- -

_____

- -

_____

- -

_____

- -

_____

- -

_____

- -

_____

- -

_____

- -

_____

- -

_____

Plurals

Choose the correct form of the plural.

City

a) citys   b) cities   c) cites   d) cityes

Book

a) bookes   b) bookies   c) books   d) book

Way

a) wayes   b) waies   c) waes   d) ways

Fox

a) foxes   b) fox   c) foxies   d) foxs

Church

a) churchs   b) churches   c) churchies   d) church

Baby

a) babys   b) babyes   c) babies   d) babes

Copywork

Copy this sentence onto the lines below: *Who makes an enemy a friend, to fear and worry puts an end.*

(This page left intentionally blank)

Matching

Some words just don't follow a rule for plurals. Use the matching game to learn some of the odd forms plurals can take. First, read through the words – the plural is to the right of each word. Then cut out the squares and mix them up, matching the word to its plural. Play it again and again until you are familiar with some of the exceptions to the plural rules!

child	children	mouse	mice
goose	geese	sheep	sheep
cactus	cacti	leaf	leaves

Copywork

Copy this sentence onto the lines below: *There the same thing happened.*

(This page left intentionally blank)

Matching

Here are some more odd plurals. Again, read through the words first – the plurals are to the right of the words. Then cut them out and mix them up. Add them to your cards from lesson 142 for a bigger challenge!

fish	fish	tooth	teeth
man	men	foot	feet
ox	oxen	person	people

Copywork

Copy this sentence onto the lines below: *A sudden odd surprise made Farmer Brown's boy's hair to rise.*

(This page left intentionally blank)

Grammar Review

Circle the nouns and underline the pronouns.

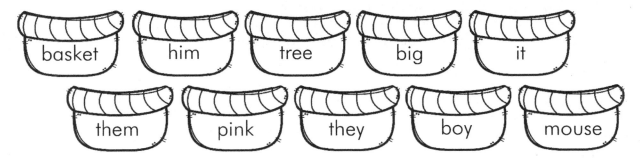

basket   him   tree   big   it

them   pink   they   boy   mouse

Fill in the punctuation mark that best fits each sentence.

I'm so excited   When is your birthday

I enjoy dancing   Help

What is your favorite food   Let's go to the park

Underline the words in each sentence that need to be capitalized.

i live in the united states of america.

what is your favorite month?

my birthday is on a saturday this year.

Copywork

Copy this sentence onto the line below: *"What is it?"*

_____

- -

_____

Long a

Fill in the blanks with the missing long A word. All of them are spelled with a silent E at the end. Can you spell them correctly?

We used the _____ to get all of the leaves into a pile.

My sister and I played a _____ of Chess.

I enjoy helping my mom _____ cupcakes.

When I visited my grandma, I flew on a _____.

My favorite flavor is _____.

Copywork

Copy this sentence onto the line below: *"That's a splendid idea!"*

Plurals

Most of the time, when a word ends in F or FE, we change the F or FE to a V and add ES to make the word plural. Rewrite the words below as a plurals in the blanks beside them.

knife _____   leaf _____

wolf _____   life _____

thief _____   half _____

wife _____   calf _____

loaf _____   shelf _____

elf _____   sheaf _____

Spelling Word Search

Find the plural words in the puzzle below. Once you find them all, have a parent or sibling read the words to you one at a time while you try to spell them.

```
W R K K C A R S Y J P R F T J
V P W P B I G E S G Y J N A M
X V B Q U B W N U E E M Z B I
E S M W A S H E S F U C O L X
O M W J Y P W O L V E S B E E
P F A T T H U E I F Z P L S S
H R T L F P S T G O I B L R C
Z K C Y Y K H K Y U W N E K L
N N H S F G E V V Y W L A W Z
E I E T X L L N S A O S V K B
V V S M O W V S X I Y J E D A
H E Y B F D E O E H Z D S D B
U S C T O Y S G R K V N Y N I
I A J V J F I G C O I X Q H E
W Q E V L I A B I K E S Y W S
```

watches	tables	cars
shelves	knives	mixes
washes	leaves	toys
wolves	bikes	babies

Plurals

Make the following words plural. As a reminder, if Y comes after a vowel, just add S. If Y comes after a consonant (any letter that's not a vowel), change the Y to I and add ES.

Write the vowels on this line for easy reference:

cherry _____   army _____

party _____   play _____

tray _____   boy _____

berry _____   fairy _____

penny_____   day _____

fly _____   copy _____

Copywork

Write a silly sentence using one or more of the words above.

Ordering Sentences

Write the words in the correct order to form a proper sentence.

have   a ball.   I

_____
- -
_____

green.   is   My ball

_____
- -
_____

bounces.   My   ball

_____
- -
_____

like   I   my ball.

_____
- -
_____

Circle the nouns below. Put a line under the proper nouns below.

pencil   Joey   green   shirt

Hawaii   far   porch   Friday

Plural Rules

The regular plural of nouns is made by adding an S to the end of the word. As we've learned, there are exceptions to this rule. We call these exceptions **irregular plurals**. Let's review what we've learned.

We make the plural of nouns that end in CH, SH, X, or SS by adding ES.

one dress	one fox	one couch
two dresses	two foxes	two couches

We make the plural of some nouns that end in F or FE by changing the F or FE to V and adding ES.

one leaf   one elf
two leaves   two elves

We make the plural of nouns that end in Y not following a vowel by changing the Y to I and adding ES.

one cherry   one fly
two cherries   two flies

We make the plural of some OO nouns by changing the OO to EE.

one foot   one goose
two feet   two geese

And of course, there are many words that just don't follow a rule.

Find the plurals:

knife _____   boy _____

box _____   miss _____

try _____   man _____

Write a sentence about your favorite place. Start it like this: *My favorite place to be is...*

_____

_____

_____

Plurals

Choose the correct form of the plural.

Child

a) childs   b) childes   c) childies   d) children

Knife

a) knifes   b) knivs   c) knives   d) knivies

Hut

a) huts   b) hutes   c) huties   d) hut

Box

a) boxs   b) boxes   c) boxies   d) boxen

Peach

a) peachs   b) peaches   c) peachies   d) peach

Lady

a) ladys   b) ladyes   c) ladies   d) lades

Mouse

a) mouses   b) mousies   c) mices   d) mice

Writing

Write a funny sentence about two of something. Use the correct form of the plural!

Plurals and Pronouns

Write the plural of each word. If you need a refresher on the rules, look at your workbook page from lesson 150. Then fill in the puzzle with the missing pronoun.

berry _____   tax _____

hatch _____   play _____

miss _____   ash _____

shelf _____   try _____

story _____   day _____

Across:
1. We went to _____ store over there.
3. Jennifer said _____ was hungry.
4. Kevin said _____ felt sick.
5. I threw the ball to Jay and he threw it back to _____.

Down:
1. Cam and Jan went shopping and I went with _____.
2. When Stu and Jeff were done _____ went home.

Spelling

Write the plurals of these words.

toy _____   leaf _____

lady _____   watch _____

bike _____

Circle the nouns below. Underline the pronouns. Color in the proper nouns.

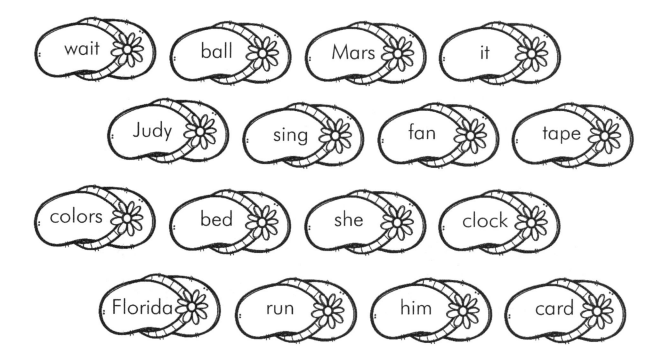

Pronouns

"Pop" the pronoun balloons. Put an X over all of the balloons that contain pronouns.

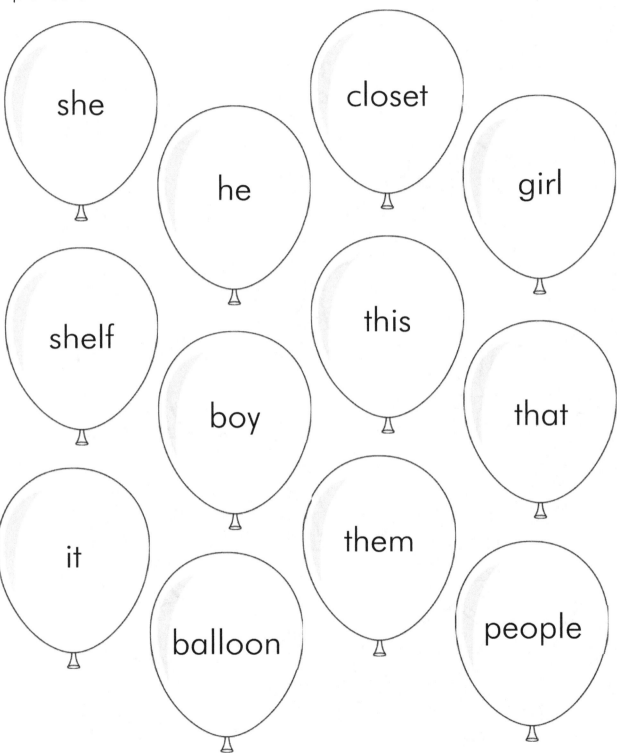

Fishing for Nouns

Color red the fish below that contain common nouns. Color blue the fish that contain pronouns.

Correct the sentences

Correct the sentences below. Remember that all sentences must begin with a capital letter and end with proper punctuation. Proper nouns should be capitalized. Just do your best and learn from any mistakes!

my favorite day is sunday

we are going to the zoo on the first friday in may

are you as excited as i am for christmas

it's freezing in here

what is your favorite color

i like folding laundry but mom doesn't

have you met my cousin, jessica

i love summer

winter is my favorite season but my mom likes spring

Plurals

Choose the correct form of the plural. You can find the rules in lesson 150, but remember there are exceptions! Learn from your mistakes if you make them.

One fox, two _____.

    a) foxs   b) foxes   c) foxies   d) foxen

One leaf, two _____.

    a) leafs   b) leavs   c) leaves   d) leavies

One lady, two _____.

    a) ladies   b) ladys   c) ladyes   d) lady

One sheep, two _____.

    a) sheeps   b) sheep   c) sheepies   d) sheepes

One church, two _____.

    a) churches   b) churchs   c) churchies   d) church

One ox, two _____.

    a) oxes   b) oxs   c) oxies   d) oxen

One kiss, two _____.

    a) kisss   b) kissies   c) kissen   d) kisses

One bird, two _____.

    a) birds   b) birdes   c) birdies   d) bird

One party, two _____.

    a) partys   b) partes   c) partyes   d) parties

One toy, two _____.

    a) toyes   b) toyes   c) toys   d) toy

What I Did Yesterday

What did you do yesterday? Be as descriptive as possible. Use complete sentences with proper capitalization and punctuation.

Pronouns

Choose the correct pronoun for each sentence. It might help to read the sentence out loud with your choice of pronoun to make sure it sounds right.

I lost my favorite shirt. Can you help _____ find it?

    a)   me   b)   my

I love my sister, but sometimes _____ fight.

    a)   she   b)   we

Katrina loves stickers. _____ has a whole collection.

    a)   She   b)   Her

That ball bounces really high, but _____ bounces higher.

    a)   my   b)   mine

James burned _____ finger on the stove.

    a)   his   b)   him

Cindy left _____ folder on the counter.

    a)   she   b)   her

Our family has two cars, but one of _____ isn't working.

    a)   it   b)   them

The Adventure Continues

Choose any book you have finished reading. Write what happens to the main character next.

_____

_____

_____

_____

_____

_____

_____

_____

_____

_____

_____

_____

_____

Writing

Write a sentence with a name in it. Be sure to capitalize the name! (Example: Liz is my friend.)

_____

_____

_____

Write another sentence, but this time replace the name with a pronoun. (Example: She makes me laugh.)

_____

_____

_____

Pop the pronoun balloons! Put an X over all of the pronouns.

she

money

you

me

think

it

bottle

we

can

him

they

that

vet

he

towel

this

Capitalization and Punctuation

Choose the proper way to write each sentence.

a. Tim has a cat   b. tim has a cat?   c. Tim has a cat.   d. Tim has a cat?

a. Jill is a girl.   b. Jill is a girl?   c. jill is a girl?   d. jill is a girl.

a. Maya is happy?   b. maya is happy   c. Maya is happy.   d. maya is happy?

a. Is Kiley sad.   b. is Kiley sad?   c. Is Kiley sad   d. Is Kiley sad?

a. are you okay.   b. Are you okay.   c. are you okay?   d. Are you okay?

a. Andy is seven.   b. andy is seven.   c. Andy is seven?   d. Andy is seven

a. is he sleeping?   b. Is he sleeping?   c. Is he sleeping.   d. is he sleeping

a. Jane is away.   b. Jane is away   c. jane is away?   d. jane is away

Word Endings

Draw a line from the egg to the right basket. Look at the word endings to help you sort.

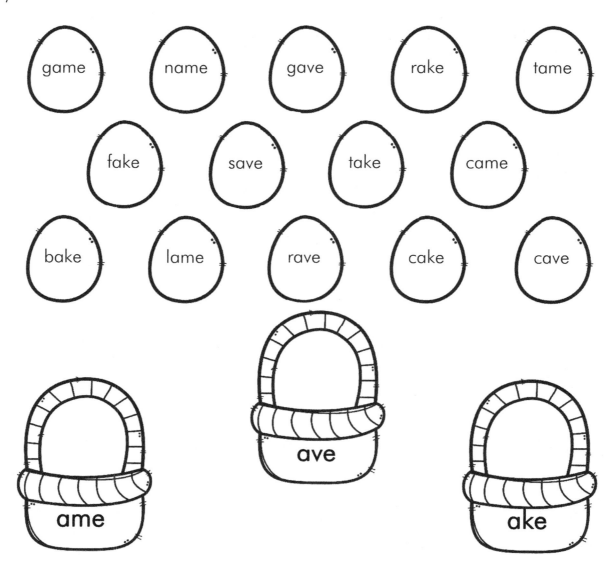

Copywork

Copy this part of the poem onto the lines below: *All things bright and beautiful*

Spelling

Choose the letter or letters from the side that best fits the blanks in the word.
Each pair is only used once.

n____l

sk____

b____k

m____t

b____t

b____s

oa

ai

ee

y

u

oo

Copywork

Copy this part of the poem onto the lines below: *All creatures great and small*

_____

_____

_____

_____

Word Builder

Choose the letters from the word box that best fit the blank within the sentences. Then go back through and circle all of the pronouns. These are long a words.

| ale | ain | raid | ai | ay |

I fell off my bike and have a p_____ in my arm.

My brother was sick and he looked p_____.

I need to m_____l a letter.

We m_____ go to the park later.

Sometimes I am af_____.

Copywork

Copy this part of the poem onto the lines below: *All things wise and wonderful*

_____
- -
_____
- -
_____

Compound Words

A **compound word** is one word made out of two words. *Bedroom* is one word but it's made from the words *bed* and *room*. Use the words from the box to make compound words out of the words listed.

| pot | road | tub | side | set | bone | boat | time |

out_____   sail_____

rail_____   wish_____

tea_____   bed_____

sun_____   bath_____

Copywork

Copy this part of the poem onto the lines below: *The Lord God made them all.*

_____

_____

_____

Word Endings

Draw a line from the egg to the right basket. Look at the word endings to help you sort.

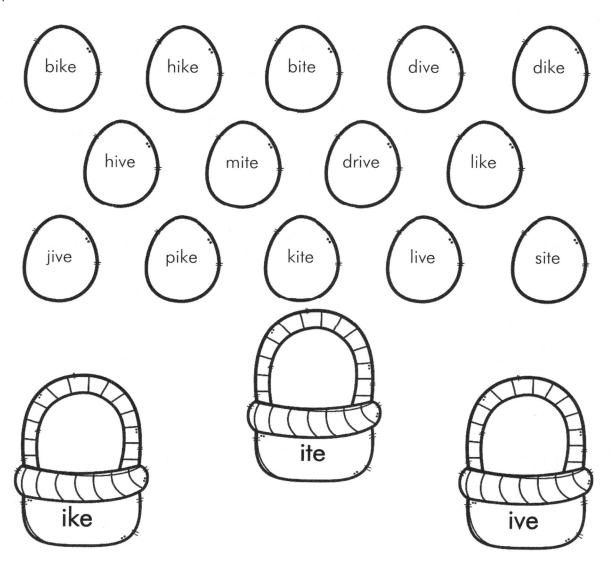

Copywork

Copy this part of the poem onto the lines below: *He gave us eyes to see them,*

_____

- -

_____

_____

- -

_____

Word Builder

Choose the letters from the box that best fit the blanks within the sentences.
Then go back through and circle all of the pronouns. These are long o words.

| oat | ow | ode | ad | now | dow |

I like to bl_____ bubbles outside.

I watched the s_____ fall.

We r_____ our bikes down the

ro_____.

The g_____ ate my carrot.

On sunny days I see my sha_____.

Copywork

Copy this part of the poem onto the lines below: *And lips that we might tell*

_____

- -

_____

- -

_____

(This page left intentionally blank)

Contractions

A **contraction** is two words combined into one. For example, *I am* becomes *I'm* as a contraction. We use an **apostrophe** in place of the letters we take out. Use this matching game to help you learn some contractions and their meanings. First, read through the words – the contraction is to the right of the words it represents. Then cut out the squares and mix them up and try to match them back again.

I have	I've	do not	don't
you will	you'll	should not	shouldn't
I am	I'm	are not	aren't

Copywork

Copy this part of the poem onto the lines below: *How great is God Almighty,*

_____

- -

_____

- -

_____

(This page left intentionally blank)

Contractions

Find which tree the contraction apple goes to. Remember that the apostrophe represents a missing letter or letters. That can help you figure out the meaning. Draw a line from the apple to the right tree.

can not   I am   you are

I'm   you're

was not   can't

haven't   I'll   I will

we're

wasn't   aren't

have not   are not   we are

Copywork

Copy this part of the poem onto the lines below: *Who has made all things well.*

Order and Comprehension

Number the boxes in the order that makes the story make sense. Then answer the questions about the story.

☐ ...except for the "crazy" part.

☐ Me too...

☐ I've had a crazy day!

What has the cat likely been doing all day?

a) resting   b) running in circles   c) working

What has the man likely been doing all day?

a) resting   b) running in circles   c) working

☐ Really? I have nothing to do.

☐ I have so much to do!

☐ I'm so late!

I'm right on time.

Why is the man late?

a) it is night   b) he has so much to do   c) his car broke down

What does the cat mean he's right on time?

a) it's morning   b) it's time for lunch   c) he has nothing to do

Plurals

Write the plural of each word. If you need a refresher on the rules, look at your workbook page from lesson 150. There are a few tricky ones!

fairy _____	elf _____
match _____	plot _____
kiss _____	sash _____
kite _____	try _____
pie _____	tray _____
knife _____	tax _____
man _____	cliff _____
foot _____	wish _____
sheep _____	game _____
itch _____	mouse _____

Noun Review

Do you remember the different kinds of nouns? Color red the common nouns. Color blue the proper nouns. Color green the pronouns. Every flower should be colored!

My Character

Draw a character of some kind. It can be anything you want. It can be silly, have any job, or not even be human – anything you want. Be creative!

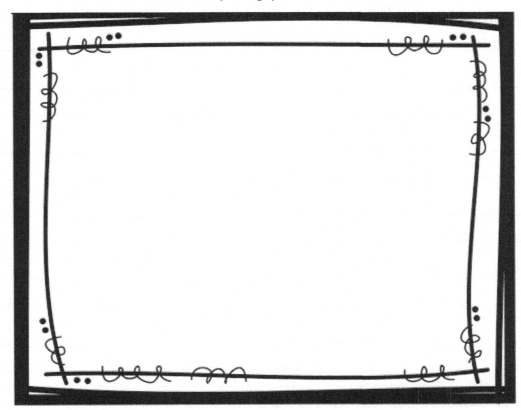

Match the picture with the word that has the same vowel sound.

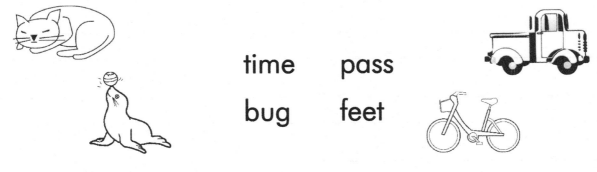

time   pass

bug   feet

Make the following words plural:

itch _____   tax _____

bike _____   stick _____

My Character

Write a short story about your character. What should we know about them? What adventures have they had? What situation did they get into today? Again, just be creative!

_____

- -

_____

- -

_____

- -

_____

- -

_____

- -

_____

- -

_____

- -

_____

- -

_____

- -

_____

- -

_____

- -

_____

- -

_____

Comic Book

Create your own comic book! If you need more sections, draw lines vertically (up and down) to further section off the rectangles. You will have more pages and more days to work on this.

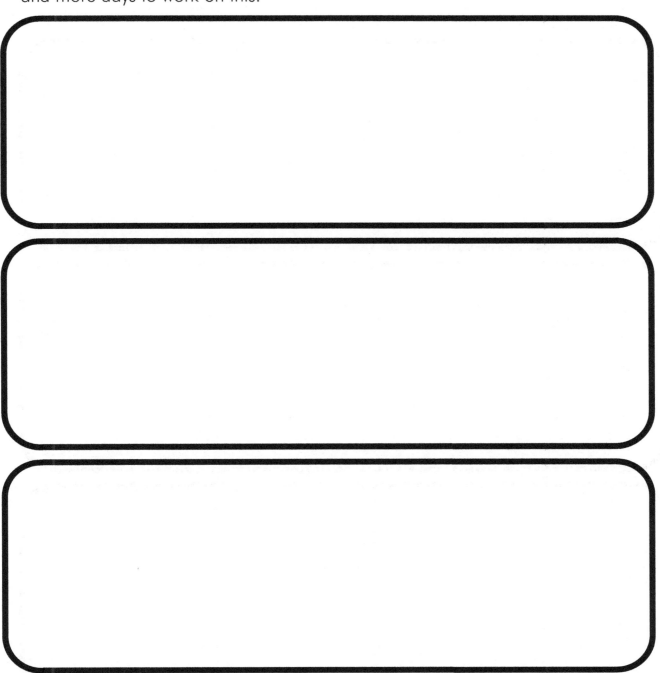

Comic Book

Continue to work on your comic book.

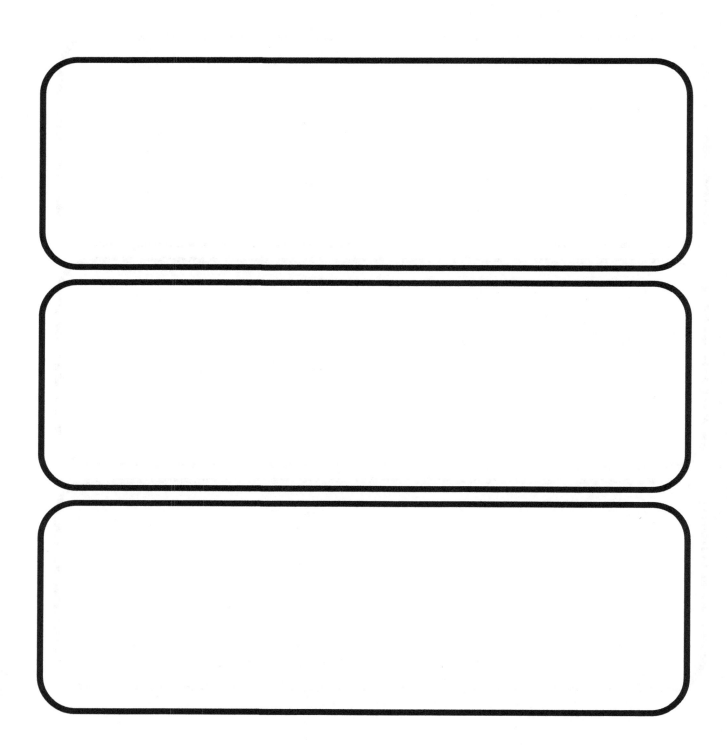

Comic Book

Continue to work on your comic book.

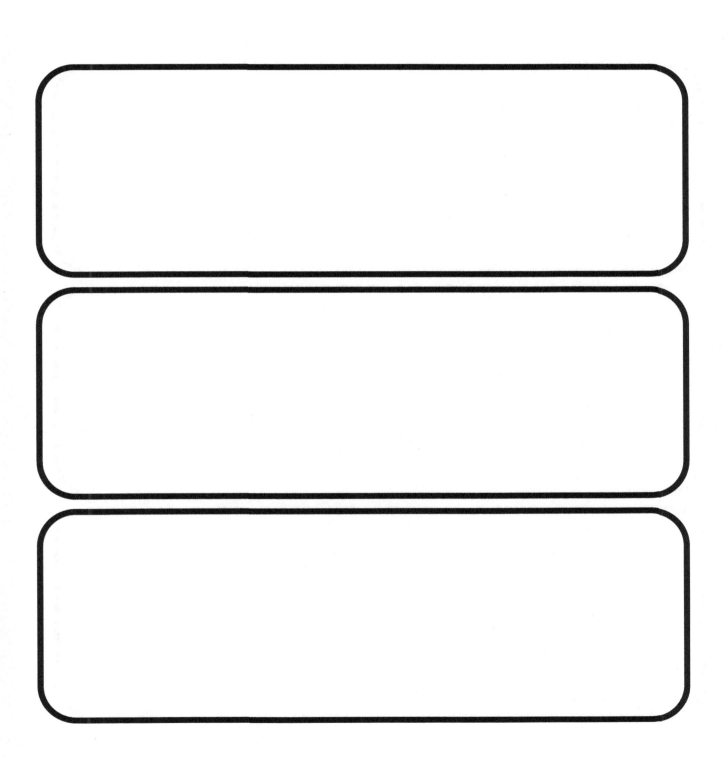

Comic Book

Continue to work on your comic book.

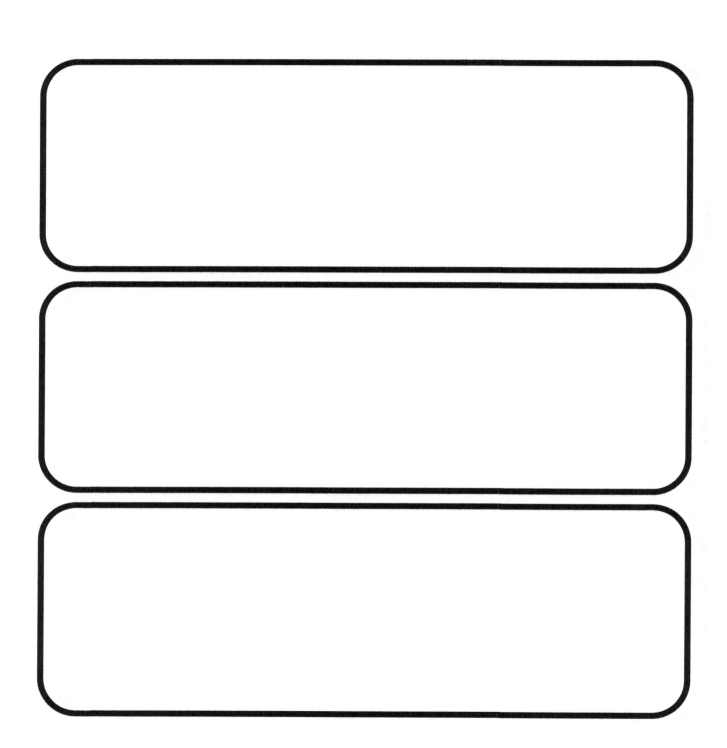

Comic Book

Finish your comic book. Read it aloud to a parent or sibling.

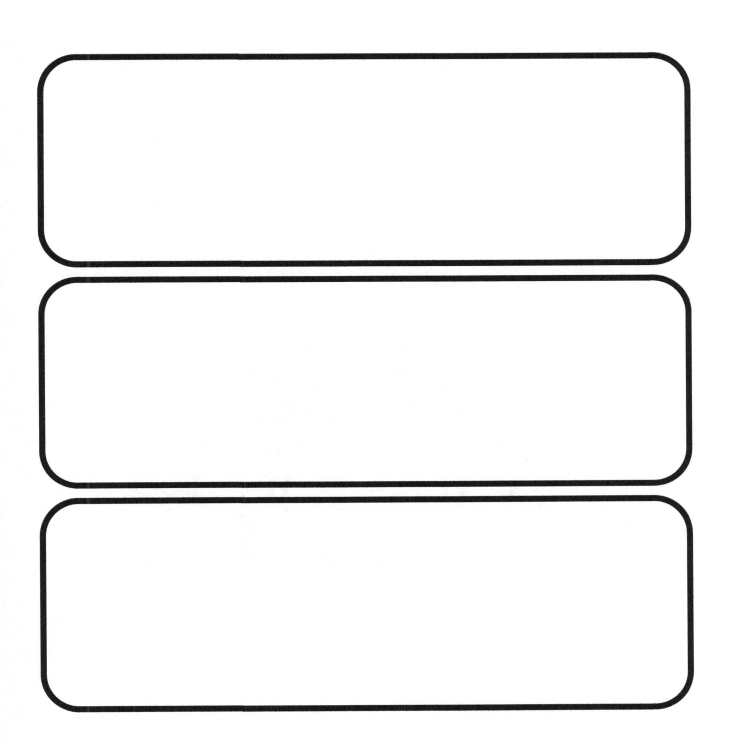

Congratulations!

You have finished Language Arts 1!

The Easy Peasy All-in-One Homeschool is a free, complete online homeschool curriculum. There are 180 days of ready-to-go assignments for every level and every subject. It's created for your children to work as independently as you want them to. Preschool through high school is available as well as courses ranging from English, math, science and history to art, music, computer, thinking, physical education and health. A daily Bible lesson is offered as well. The mission of Easy Peasy is to enable those to homeschool who otherwise thought they couldn't.

The Genesis Curriculum takes the Bible and turns it into lessons for your homeschool. Daily lessons include Bible reading, memory verse, spelling, handwriting, vocabulary, grammar, Biblical language, science, social studies, writing, and thinking through discussion questions.

The Genesis Curriculum uses a complete book of the Bible for one full year. The curriculum is being made using both Old and New Testament books. Find us online at genesiscurriculum.com to read about the latest developments in this expanding curriculum.